becoming remarkable

"Encouraging others to write with honesty and intelligence, Harriet shares her insights generously, revealing the strong and sensitive character that emerges in her own songwriting. I return to her articles frequently for sustenance and inspiration."

Arthur Schlosser
Songwriter

"Ms. Schock's writing is uncluttered, intelligent, and honest. Full of compassion and insight, her ideas are grounded in a compelling reality, what she calls 'the power and logic of reality to keep the song on course.' As her subjects range from issues of gender to notions of literacy, her writing remains tough-minded and graceful. If you ever thought of writing a song or a poem, write it with this book in hand."

Steve Wyckoff, Department of English
Lehman College, New York

"In a business so deeply rooted in illusion and hype, it's quite refreshing to have the kind of splash-some-cold-water-on-your-face honesty that Harriet has given us in this book. She seems to have gotten to the basics of what it's like to really feel, communicate, touch, and write from the heart. It made me remember why I started doing this songwriting thing in the first place. Read it and be remarkable!"

Michael Duff
Chalk FarM

becoming remarkable

for songwriters
and those who love songs

harriet schock

BLUE DOLPHIN PUBLISHING

Published by
Blue Dolphin Publishing, Inc.
P.O. Box 8, Nevada City, CA 95959
Orders: 1-800-643-0765
http://www.bluedolphinpublishing.com

ISBN: 1-57733-050-1

Library of Congress Cataloging-in-Publication Data

Schock, Harriet.
    Becoming remarkable : for songwriters and those who love songs /
Harriet Schock.
        p.   cm.
    Contains previously published articles.
    ISBN 1-57733-050-1
    1. Popular music—writing and publishing. I. Music.
MT67.S33 1998
782-4264'13—dc21   98-39921
                                                              CIP
                                                               MN

Cover art: photo courtesy of Evening*Star Music Group
Index by Brackney Indexing Service

Printed in the United States of America

10   9   8   7   6   5   4   3   2   1

This book is dedicated to Nik Venet

On a page in my date book marked Monday, December 5, 1977, I have a note to myself that says, "Call Nick Venay." I had written phonetically the name left on my answering machine when he called me that day. In Nik Venet's date book, in that same month, my name is written, spelled correctly. It would be 13 years and three months before we met, face to face, at a NARAS local board of Governors' meeting. Six years after that, he showed me the page from his book. He had written, "Harriet Schock—the Georgia O'Keeffe of songwriters." I never really understood what that meant, but I knew he liked Georgia O'Keeffe, so that was enough for me.

Nik Venet believed that with every song, the songwriter should become a better person, because he or she is writing from truth and discovering and uncovering life in the process of writing. It ultimately became impossible for me to differentiate between what I learned from the process of writing and what I learned from the process of writing under Nik Venet's influence. I suspect it was the latter that changed me the most.

Naturally, many of the beliefs Nik Venet embraced about songwriting, I already believed. That's one reason it was such a good creative match. But much of it I had abandoned between the years 1975, when my third album was released, and 1991, when Nik produced my fourth one. Briefly, I had forgotten who I was as a writer/artist. Nik reminded me. And because someone actually seemed to want to hear what I had to say, I allowed myself to grow as a writer. And I took the gag from my mouth, the rope from my hands, and started communicating again.

Having produced such wonderful writers as Dory Previn, Fred Neil, Brian Wilson, Bobby Darin, and Jim Croce, Nik understood how to get songs out of writers. He also could tell the minute a writer was disconnected from his or her writing, even in one line.

What Nik did for me and my writing was a gift to my soul. It is my hope that when I come into contact with a songwriter, I can help him or her find and communicate that truth that is uniquely his or hers. Writers look at the world a little askew, and that viewpoint helps others see it more clearly.

I will always see the world differently from knowing Nik Venet. And I will see it as a more fascinating place, a more fertile and a sweeter place because of the seven years I had with him.

Table of Contents

Foreword

My father originally intended to write the foreword to this book. Because he passed away in January, 1998, he was not able to. In March, I found this piece among his writings and correspondences. It's less about Harriet, the teacher and author, than it is about the writer/artist. But as my father always said, it's impossible to separate the two anyway, in her case. Her teaching is an art and in her art, she teaches.

—Nik Venet, Jr.

WHAT SHE DOES NOT KNOW is as important as what she does know. She does not know she collects. She does not know why she protects and holds all the small things that make her Harriet.

Harriet never noticed the things she collected the way I notice it. I wanted to tell her, often, quietly and without asking her to respond. I just wanted to hear my voice place these words into her writing universe. Like a gift to her for being who she is as a being, at that very moment. To most eyes the clutter of objects may have seemed like ordinary junk, broken parts, odd things with nowhere else to be stored. With eyes like mine, that watched her dance out of a room, sing to herself while writing, laugh when she had been fooled, my eyes saw these things as sacred objects. Surrounded by circumstance, the drawers were small boxes in the tradition of the Ark of the Covenant . . . all bundled and stashed like Emily Dickinson's forty-nine bound packets of poems, found stashed in a dresser drawer. Carefully written and stored, her sacred writings were also preserved with ritual ribbons tied around odd scarves. Her books of notes and Harriet's boxes of sacred clutter were like birds in search of a cage.

Harriet has enough of the past stashed, bound, and wrapped like notes, for a volume of dreams. A heart saving diary, an album of photographs, small locked boxes that no longer unlock, small unlocked boxes that no longer lock, like lovers separated by small indifferences, all containing the same sum of parts. All of her somethings, saved in a small, sweet, significant way, making everything once common sacred.

All these things are so far removed from the human situation as to be almost worthless to a lesser spirited person. Harriet has saved all of it, as if she were collecting the butterfly wings from points in time. A small diary in metaphoric and symbolic short-hand. Part of her future songs and past proof of a heart's many instant decisions and reasons to keep the bird's cage door open.

Harriet's infinite inner space of song story line, whether from her religion or from a common experience, is its soul. Most songwriters deprive the story of their mystery, leaving the listener with an empty box of fact, one level of a single meaning. Schock, as a literate and practiced professional, allows the song its soul, so we can discover our own depths through it. Most students, through their writing, blame their parents for everything they have become. Schock changes the situation by seeing through the child-hood stories, writing through the self-made myth, pulling out their poetry, and allowing the mysteries of it all to sing through the lyric.

Schock, in her songs, never becomes the main character of her songs. She does not allow herself to become the current cultural definition of her art. Her soul is more interested in particulars than in generalities. She brings order to her imaginings, like her saved clutter of mementos, she writes order to her chaos of life. Each person, in each verse, in every song that she writes has a special story to tell, no matter how many common themes are contained in her songs.

It is never easy to work with an artist like Harriet Schock. It is work. But care of the soul requires work. The songs we work on come from that place we would rather not visit, but that is the most honest place to find a song. Looking in that place in ourselves will always give the songwriter the true, naked image of the concept. The work may be intense, but it is also the source of the songwriter's soul.

My father often told me that dreams are the mythology of the soul, and working with them, as an artist, makes life more artful.

As a producer, I prefer to work with Harriet Schock as a songwriter, writer, and artist, because each of her songs tells the story of a soul rather than a life. I believe in her and I believe in her truth. I am always honored to be a small part of greatness.

Nik Venet
July 19, 1996

About the Chapters...

I organized the forty-eight chapters as follows:

1. Integrity (articles that emphasize WHY songwriters express)

2. Clarity (articles that emphasize WHAT songwriters express

3. Technology (articles that emphasize HOW songwriters express).

I realize that many of the chapters contain all three aspects; I decided to place them in one category over the others by which aspect was emphasized the most.

I offer this as a fresh way for us to look at this wonderful material; I hope that it is useful. The wisdom, encouragement and practical insights that Harriet Schock communicates so clearly have helped me to become a better songwriter and a better person.

—Naomi Healing

Acknowledgments

I'D LIKE TO THANK John Braheny for asking me to write, regularly, about songwriting for the *Los Angeles Songwriters Showcase Musepaper*, later published by the National Academy of Songwriters. Over twenty other cities subsequently asked to publish these writings in their songwriters' periodicals.

This accomplished a number of things for me: It put me in touch with songwriters all over the world, many of whom became my private students. It also helped me chronicle my thoughts on, observations of, and discoveries about songwriting from May 1991 to March 1997. More importantly, it helped me chronicle many observations of Nik Venet's, which can be found in almost every chapter of this book.

I also very much appreciate the work of my editor, Naomi Healing, who had the original vision and desire to organize the book into chapters as you see here and to provide the chapter topic guide. She did the job with the kind of caring, wisdom, and sensitivity that she applies to all parts of life.

I'd like to thank Mitch Santell, who brought the manuscript to Blue Dolphin, and Paul Clemens and Linda Maxwell at Blue Dolphin for all their work in getting this book out and into your hands.

And finally, I'm extremely grateful to the songwriters whose lyrics I quote in these pages. Many excellent novelists, poets, screenwriters, and songwriters have contributed to my growing understanding of what "becoming remarkable" means. Those who were not mentioned by name may simply not have come to mind to illustrate a point in the writing of these chapters.

Introduction

SOME PEOPLE BELIEVE that art and commercial success are in conflict, and sometimes they are, but I believe one does not necessarily preclude the other. This book is not about becoming a financial success through songwriting. It's about becoming remarkable. Sometimes those things coincide, as in the case of great songwriter/artists like Joni Mitchell, Don Henley, Bob Dylan to name just a few. Time will tell which of the newer writers are true artists and which ones are chasing the tail of the music industry.

I've observed two things about remarkable songwriters. 1) They come from truth. I don't mean their songs are necessarily factual, but they always contain truth (see Chapter 18, "Truth vs. Fact in Songwriting"). The truth simply has more emotional impact because when the writer writes it, it has a ring of authenticity, and when the listener hears it, it has a ring of veracity, both musically and lyrically. Telling the truth as an artist can be a lifelong pursuit as the truth reveals itself more and more by the lives we lead. 2) They have mastered the language of songwriting and can speak it fluently. This mastery is also not an overnight endeavor, but like any language, there are certain principles and techniques that can be applied to expedite the process. Both of these ingredients seem to be necessary for remarkable writing. Without fluency in the language of songwriting, writing from truth can seem self-indulgent and downright embarrassing. Without the truth, the master craftsman only crafts another good song, which will not deeply touch anyone's life and will not be remembered.

I hope I am still traveling on the road to becoming remarkable. I also hope that the observations I've made on this road will help bring you a few steps closer to that glorious, elusive destination.

Part I

Integrity

1

Step One:
Touch Somebody

*T*HINK BACK TO THE FIRST TIME you wrote a song for someone and then played it for that person. Did it have an effect on him or her? And wasn't that a thrill? At that moment, you may have realized that the whole thing is about communication. And if it was real enough to make someone smile, or cry, or say "thank you," then who knows? It might be real enough to move millions of other people.

I live in a duplex. My only contact with the upstairs neighbors had been when I discovered my music room was directly under one of their bedrooms. Being quite elderly, they go to bed at about 9:30, so I moved my music studio to another room, directly under their spare room. They were very grateful and sweet about it. Last week, I called them to ask them something about the television antenna. They invited me up for fruit. I spent an hour and a half hearing them speak of their life, their many pets through the years, their children and grandchildren. I was so moved by the experience, I couldn't stop thinking and feeling about it. So I started writing. . . .

3

"The television looks like it's from the fifties,
Except that there's a cable in the back.
He sits in his special chair,
Half awake and half aware
That she is in the room somewhere,
That is his pivotal fact."

I realized that, in the middle of a million things I was supposed to be doing, I was writing a song about my upstairs neighbors. Not knowing them very well, I didn't know how they would feel about having their love story immortalized by the night owl below them, but I knew I was hooked and couldn't stop.

I called them up and told the wife I had written a song of tribute to her relationship with her husband. She then said one of those things that will forever stay in my memory, not only as a comment, but as a life's lesson. She said, "Well, it certainly can't harm the relationship. Everything only makes it better." I knew, at that point, here was a lady who had made some sane decisions. I really wanted her to like the song.

They came down this morning and I played it for them. They smiled and thanked me. Then she asked me to read the lyric to her. I did. We had a nice visit and they left. They had asked me for a copy of the lyric, which I gave them. But I made them promise when their children and grandchildren heard it, they'd let me play it with the melody, not just read the lyric. They agreed. Ten minutes after they left, the wife called me and told me that after she read the lyric, she realized what it said, how moved she was, and that her husband had tears in his eyes as well. They just couldn't hear quite well enough to make out the words without reading them. Then she said she didn't know how she could ever thank me enough for what I had done. And I thought to myself, I should be thanking them for the inspiration. What a rare couple it is who can instill that kind of feeling in someone.

My point here is that, yes, it's exciting when I hear a song of mine on the radio or in a film for the first time. But that's sort of a wild excitement that's directed outward. I've actually been known to go up to bikers in restaurants and tell them my song was playing, only to be thrilled that they were actually familiar with it and equally pleased that they weren't offended I had spoken to them. But the kind of reward I'm talking about is of a deeper, more inward nature. It comes from playing a personal communication to someone.

It's such a wonderful gift to be able to put something into music and words in the first place. And to offer it to someone as a validation of something he or she did—that's really quite a gift also. And if you've never done it, you're really missing something. On my second album, I had a song called "Mama," which was covered by Helen Reddy, after she'd had a hit with "Ain't No Way to Treat a Lady." When Helen was touring, she went through Dallas, and my mother went to see her. Afterward, my mother proudly announced that she was the "Mama" the song was written about. Looking back now, I'm so happy I had the foresight to write that song when I did.

So, as I tell every class I teach and every seminar I give, there are many reasons to write songs. Getting on the charts is just one of them, and usually not a very inspiring goal. Money is cold and generally doesn't get the kind of juices flowing that inspire art. But there are many lives to be touched by the gifts we have as songwriters. You might find that giving one of these gifts is as rewarding to you as to the recipient, if not more so.

2

If You're Doing It for the Money, You May Not Make Any

SOMETIMES I HAVE TO PINCH MYSELF and remind myself it isn't Kansas anymore—or wherever I came from way, way back, when I formed the belief that everyone shot straight from the hip, or at least straight.

Last week, one of my Advanced Class students said something which has bothered me ever since. It's not that I haven't heard it before—in fact, I've heard it much too often—but usually from business executives, and jaded ones at that.

The whole thing started when I commented that a number of songs on the radio recently have sounded quite a lot like another song called, "Old Time Rock & Roll." The student defended them with the statement that they were making money from these clones. I suggested that integrity might enter the picture somewhere (he was a new student, so I was more tactful than I might have been on his 4th week). To this he responded with the line in question, "Integrity doesn't pay the bills."

First of all, I can understand the attention a person might have on paying the bills, especially in this economy. But I feel it's such an incredibly dangerous viewpoint for an artist to have, I wanted to address it—or undress it—publicly. The student who said it is talented and bright, and I don't think he actually embraces this as a heartfelt philosophy. I think it was an offhanded remark. But since he said it, here goes.

Check out the definition of "integrity." It's not just honesty or incorruptibility. It's also "wholeness," "soundness." It's in the writer's nature to put things together to form a whole—and that's the main meaning of "integrate." I've observed many writers—colleagues, mentors, students—some hugely successful, some total unknowns. But one thing I've noticed is that the ones who are doing it because they love it and have something to express are generally the ones being successful at it. The ones who got into it to make money usually never did. It's sort of like a guy who takes a girl out just to go to bed with her and can't figure out why he never gets to.

It's not that you're getting punished for being mercenary, or anything else so linearly Puritan. It's simply that you're coming from the wrong place and that's where your attention will be—on the money, not on the music. You'll make decisions based on that; your passion will be centered somewhere away from the song. It's like trying to get turned on by the person you married for money. You've created your own prison.

Now somewhere, some songwriter is reading this who has made a lot of money with his/her art and he/you may be smiling. But think back to when you first started writing. Weren't you doing it for the love of the process, the heat of the communication, the thrill of the music? And when your attention is on writing "something that will sell," do you like what you come up with as well as you do when you write because you really want to say something or get that musical idea on tape?

I have heard my producer, Nik Venet, say that even though McDonald's may be the biggest restaurant chain, one would not ask to meet and compliment the chef there. Similarly, *Citizen Kane* never made its investment back, whereas *Love Story* made millions. But which one do we remember?

In my own experience, songs I wrote from that burning desire to communicate were always my most successful copyrights. And here I'm talking about songwriting—not assignment writing for films or records, because that's a whole different subject. They are commissioned anyway. I'm referring to those songs that are an extension of who you are as an artist—that you would perform yourself, proudly, if you sing.

"Integrity doesn't pay the bills" may be true. But neither does chasing trends, writing at the radio, ripping off other songs, and focusing on writing something that will make a lot of money. To make a lot of money, it has to sell a lot or be played a lot or both. That means lots of people have to hear it and buy it. That means it has to move people when they hear it. Now, if you think you're good enough to write something that's going to move all those people, while you've got your attention and your passion over there on your bank statement, be my guest. Give it a try. But your craft had better be unbelievably good to pull that one off. And between the time you start and the time your craft is THAT good, there's a lot of dues paying and songwriting you'll have to do. So you might just as well do it for the love of it. Maybe you'll even discover in the process that integrity has fewer bills to pay.

3

The Art & Craft
of Songwriting

I'VE RECENTLY COME TO THE VIEWPOINT that it's necessary to understand all art in order to understand any art. I've noticed that
people who have an appreciation for the visual arts, literature,
dance, etc. also approach music in a more vulnerable way. And,
conversely, those who are virtually illiterate, and pride themselves on the fact that television is the height of their artistic
appetites, may even make a living in music, but they appear to be
unmoved by it, unchanged by it and approach it as a product, in
much the way the commercials they watch deal with their products.

As my writer friend, Thomas Lane, pointed out after looking
up the derivation of "art," the word comes from "ars artis" meaning to join together. His "Artist Manifesto" is being published
shortly and it makes a very strong point about the necessity of
artists in all areas to join together. He also places the responsibility
for the condition of the arts back into the hands of the artists—
which will rob us of our self-righteous whining and give us a
pretty huge job to do.

9

Reading Tom's Artist Manifesto had a powerful effect on me, as it will all of you when you read it. And combined with the recent inspiration I have experienced by listening to the National Academy of Songwriters Gold Songwriters showcase at Genghis Cohen, I am beginning to believe those around me who insist we are at the threshold of a Renaissance in the music business. I certainly hope this is true, not only for selfish reasons, but because of the quality of songwriting I see around me, from my colleagues, my students, my friends.

I was pondering this possibility when I heard a statement from my producer, Nik Venet, which I feel I must quote. In fact, I keep it at eye level much of the time when I'm writing, or singing. It goes like this:

"Everyone writes.
Everyone sings.
Not everyone tells the truth.
It's the truth that touches people."

—Nik Venet

He just said it in the studio, in passing, when he was trying to get me to perform the songs we're cutting, LIVE, and by that I mean playing and singing at the same time in a total performance, as opposed to overdubbing and making it "all perfect." You have to remember, I'm from the South (or Southwest if that's where you consider Dallas to be) and I was brought up on advice like, "Look your best even when you're breaking up with him," so you can imagine how hard it's been for Nik Venet to convince me to do things live. It sometimes feels like I'm being asked to stand in my underwear in bright sunlight with no make-up on. Sure it's real, but so is a train wreck.

I recently read a quote from the London Times that discussed the John Stewart Phoenix Live album, also produced by Nik, that has re-charted this month in England. John voiced the same insecurities when Nik first urged him to release it, "flaws and all" because it's real, it's human, and it's truthful. The effect it created and is creating again is amazing. I suppose if it had been over-dubbed to make the performers feel good, the listener would have felt much less.

But back to the point I opened with—that of appreciating all art in order to really "get into" one form of art. I went to an exhibit of Modern Art, yesterday, at the county museum on Wilshire and I studied two paintings by John Singer Sargent. I was completely awed by them. In order for him to create the picture you get when you stand across the room, from the close distance where he painted it, he had to have the craft down totally cold, and then he had to be so free of the craft, he could express himself directly and communicate without attention to technique. As songwriters, that's the point we must arrive at, so that we don't pull the listener into our struggle with the form, or into our cleverness with it. When I mentioned all this to Venet, he faxed me a transcript someone took off a tape of a lecture he delivered at UCLA in 1984, where he taught record production to a class that achieved some renown for having started with 30 enrolled, and having ended up with over 300.

This quote actually says exactly what I want to say on the subject, so rather than paraphrasing, I'll just give it verbatim:

"Sampled, crystal clear records, void of the human condition, cannot compare with a live performance captured on tape or a real-life experience placed on paper . . . to be sung from the heart. Only a few have the bravery to do it honestly, using their years of dues-paying craft study to free their fingers and voice from the mind . . . so that the soul, without obstruction of form, dictates the words, music and paint strokes and how they will be shared."

The entire transcript of this speech is phenomenal, but I wanted to quote salient parts of it here, because it articulated beautifully something I've been trying to say to my advanced students, in answer to the sometimes unspoken question, "When is it finished? When am I good enough? When can I stop working at it and just enjoy it? What is craft, anyway? And what is art?"

So our job is to become good enough at the Craft that we can become free to engage in the Art, and take enough responsibility for the Condition of the Arts to make sure there's someone out there capable of not just hearing—but listening. And once we know they're listening, to give them the truth.

4

Songwriters . . .
A Community

A FEW NIGHTS AGO, I received a fax of a newspaper article from my producer, Nik Venet. It was a short write-up of Marlene Dietrich's funeral. And the information in it got me to drop everything and go to the piano and write a song about it. I was very moved. Maybe you'll see why.

One of our great movie stars, after gaining fame abroad, came to this country and made films. She left Germany because she disagreed with Hitler's politics long before World War II. She also sang in films and recorded for a major American label. After a while, she left. She did a good job and she merely exited. But Hollywood didn't like that. In a town that is accustomed to having its stars vanish by unexplained death, or protest against obscurity by groveling in horror films, or hide in plain sight with layers of camouflage . . . simply leaving L.A. with her integrity intact was an inexcusable crime.

How do we know Hollywood felt this way? Not one person from the film industry showed up at the funeral. No flowers. No cards. And, needless to say, the record business was not represented either. There are only two possible explanations. Either they forgot about her after she left, or they were offended. Either explanation is not okay with me.

Of course, no one likes to be preached to in a song, and I felt like getting my point across, so I assumed the viewpoint of the town and addressed the song to Ms. Dietrich.

"In the city of the angels
Where nobody gets blue
We have a vague recollection
Of someone like you
But we couldn't make the funeral
We had so much to do, Marlene. . .
I think that was your name."

The reason I titled this article "Songwriters . . . A Community" is that I feel a real sense of caring between songwriters. All you have to do is be in the NAS office for a few hours to see how much of a community we really have. And the annual Salute to the American Songwriter recognizes the importance of songwriters' works, whether they're local or not. Naturally, Nashville has a thriving songwriters' community, and the Hall of Fame acknowledges the work of great writers who may have passed away long before many of our contemporaries were even born.

But I'm afraid "Hollywood" doesn't value its own in the same way.

"Yes, our stars are best at shining
With their backs against the wall
And we sometimes see them broken
And sometimes see them crawl
But we're certain to forget them
If we don't see them at all, Marlene
I think that was your name."

It's not that Hollywood doesn't honor its greats, but merchandising aside, if someone isn't currently making money for them, the memory cells may lose their motivation. And a trip to Paris or Berlin (there were funeral ceremonies in both cities) is a hefty plane fare to put on an expense account.

"We have our Garbo
Coat, and scarf and shades
And Norma Jean
Her mystery never fades
We have Princess Grace
With her perfect face
Why do we need you?
You broke the rules. . . ."

The creative community has traditionally been more caring than the business community. And this is just another example. An article in the New Yorker had ignited a fire in the writer whose column I read, who ignited one in me. Now, when I perform this song, I will be paying tribute to an artist whose art and life were on her own terms. And hopefully, I will inspire someone else to a higher awareness of Marlene Dietrich, and all that she represents.

The columnist I read ended with the words, "When Dietrich's movie career ended, not only her legend but she herself grew. No wonder Hollywood turned its back on her at the last; she was the one who really got away."

When I'm in New Mexico this weekend, I'm going to be thinking about that statement. And when I do, I'll be glad once again that I'm a member of the American songwriting community and not of Hollywood. I might just come back.

5

Do We Know
Where We're Coming From?

I FIND, IN TALKING TO PROSPECTIVE STUDENTS and other songwriters, there are those who respect roots and those who have no idea of them. Some of them, like my current student and friend, Mark Islam, know more about who wrote what in the past than I do. They're walking encyclopedias of songwriter credits. And I find that the kind of writing these people do is usually richer, more impactful and less derivative, strangely enough, than the writing of those who have ignored what came before.

Some songwriters I talk to boast that they never listen to the radio or records; they don't want to be influenced by what anyone else has done. They just haven't had the benefit of choosing something they really love and analyzing what's great about it—playing it, letting it run through them and being affected by it. What they may not realize is that, while they're shopping for groceries or riding in an elevator, they're hearing melodies from the thirties, forties, fifties, sixties, seventies, eighties and nineties being piped in. So they're being influenced, but not by choice.

Recently I was working with a rock group of eighteen-year-olds. The songwriter of the group admitted his main influences

16

were Stevie Wonder and Joni Mitchell. I was impressed. Then the guitar player unfortunately opened his mouth when the name, Don Henley, was mentioned and tossed off some sort of un-thought-out derogatory remark. As most of my colleagues know, anyone who speaks disparagingly of Don Henley around me counts himself lucky if he lives long enough to be humiliated by my response. I'm proud to say I allowed the guitar player to live.

I've thought a lot about why songwriters sometimes ignore the great talents that preceded them. Picasso copied the masters of realism when he first started painting. He was fascinated by them. Even up to the end of his life he continued to sketch, realistically. His style was, therefore, from choice. Some songwriters I know write the way they do because they have no choice. They literally cannot duplicate something they've heard. So they are like an artist who splashes paint on the canvas because that's all he can do. He couldn't draw a table anyway, so he just throws paint. Such a person is an impostor in a way. He's infiltrated an art form and is trying to pass as a "contemporary" artist.

As outside as this may sound, I really think this phenomenon of ignoring musical roots has to do with the disintegrating com-munication within families. When I was growing up, I learned songs my father taught me (as Linda Ronstadt did). He'd play the marimba and I'd play the piano. Before I taught him the Beatles and Ray Charles, he had taught me Hoagy Carmichael, Cole Porter, and Rogers and Hart. I was too young to know what "old fashioned" meant. So, I lucked into having a rich, melodic back-ground before I started plunking out my original ideas and devel-oping "attitude." I guess in a family where the parents are cau-tioned to be "seen and not heard," their music gets ignored along with their philosophies.

Even though I've talked a lot in here about songwriters who ignore their artistic heritage, I still maintain they're in the minor-ity. Certainly, they are the minority of successful songwriters. I think if you went out and surveyed songwriters who make a living at it, they'd all have their favorite legends they listen to and continue to be influenced by. And, of course, these influences may change over a lifetime and a career.

It's so appropriate for the National Academy of Songwriters to have an Annual Salute to the American Songwriter, where many decades of songwriters are honored and brought out from behind the scenes into the limelight. As I write this, it is three days before the Salute, which I am thrilled to be performing at this year. But an equal thrill is to be in the audience, watching and listening to songs that raised the hair on my neck in high school . . . to songs that delighted me before I knew what a pre-chorus was . . . to songs that got me dancing, crying, calling my girlfriends, leaving my boyfriends, playing by ear and wanting to be a songwriter. Not to know these songs is like calling yourself an architect and saying "Frank Lloyd who?"

6

Stop and Look
at Who's Listening

AVE YOU EVER SEEN A SAILBOAT tacking into the wind? No one with any definite destination would ever consider just getting into a sailboat and letting the wind decide. It's a constant process of correcting and correcting. Eventually the wind takes the boat where the sailor wants to go.

Why is it any different with songs? We start with a first draft (no pun intended). We show it to someone we trust. By his/her response, we discover whether we've accomplished what we intended with the communication. This was pointed up clearly at a recent seminar at which I was a guest speaker. It was easy to see which songs had true emotional impact and which ones were depending on a vocal quality or a rhythm track to communicate at all. The most effective ones, of course, were those which communicated something universally felt, exactly as the writer intended, in both melody and lyrics, and this communication was strengthened by the track and the vocal. Others were almost there, but there was something in one part—melody, lyric or chord progression—which was crippling the rest of the song.

There was one song in which a woman was the central character. Most of the people disliked her by the time the song was over. The consensus was that the melody and track were working but that no one would want to be identified with this character enough to sing the song. The woman in the song was living out a situation which happens a lot, but it was presented in a way that made her look like she had no integrity or courage, was a victim and a complainer. I questioned the writers why the character did what she did, and they pointed to one line in a verse that turned out to be a clue to the solution. I suggested some new lines in the bridge which would expound on the idea which was buried in the verse. When the seminar was over, they brought me the new bridge. They took my suggestions for lines in the bridge, giving the character a redeeming quality which made her human, likable, and someone with whom many of us could identify.

I was surprised to discover after this incident that, although people show their songs all the time, they rarely come out of the experience with a rewrite or even a direction for one. Apparently, what usually happens is this: A songwriter goes to a pitch session. The person listening is a publisher or A&R rep. For the most part— and there are some exceptions which I'll get to—these critiquers are not writers. They are business people. Their job is to sell. They are looking for something they can sell. They may have a firm idea of what that is through past experience, parameters given them by their employer, etc. So they're listening for a sound or for something that seems to be salable and will enhance their income or position or both. They provide the wind part of the sailboat analogy. They can't tell you how to move the sail to go where you want to go; they just know what they want (hopefully). Their wind blows pretty much in one direction all the time. It's your job (with any songwriting coach you may be using) to get the song into shape, so that it will at least say what you want, both lyrically and melodically, and tack into the wind to take you to your destination. Sometimes that destination is just to make a good impression on this person, so that next time you'll be heard and not ignored.

So often a student will make a remark to me like, "I can't have any words that repeat in the song. No repetition." I'll ask where they ever heard such a thing, and it will invariably trace back to one of these pitch sessions. Riddled with and inhibited by "You can't do that in a song," they're even farther away from writing a song that will affect someone emotionally. Sometimes it's the songwriter himself who has made the rule based on something the critiquer has said. Sometimes it's the publisher/A&R rep who's giving out this not-so-helpful advice. But, from what I've seen, all these rules really clutter up the creative process. Such critiquers would serve the songwriter better by merely passing on the song. When they start suggesting what's wrong with it, they frequently do more harm than good, giving bogus, if well-intended advice. If Neil Simon had a scene that wasn't working, I don't think he'd go to his agent for advice. It's as simple as that.

I mentioned earlier that there were some exceptions to publishers and A&R people being mainly on the selling side, rather than the creating side. One of these is Tony Berg, a very well-respected producer who is now in A&R at Geffen. He's a musician, composer, and songwriter and exceptionally well-qualified to comment on songs. He used to be the only person I would go to with a new song, and his comments were always insightful and inspiring. Nik Venet also has an uncanny ability to hear a song and not only find what might make it stronger, but also to see into its future—where it belongs, how it should be dressed, and to whom it should be presented. And I don't mean matching it up with artists only. I also mean finding its audiences, surrounding it with the right songs on an album or in a live set—creative vision of that nature. This vision could also account for his finding or getting written and producing the right vehicles for launching the careers of Linda Ronstadt, The Beach Boys, Bobby Darin, Jim Croce, John Stewart, Lou Rawls. Dory Previn, and all the rest. Both of these producers are well-versed in all the arts, not just the recording arts.

There are some people on the business side who have quite a lot of things to say to us. But they are still coming from a creative place. It's sort of like the role of an editor in literature. You may have heard of Maxwell Perkins, who had a larger role in the lives of Hemingway, Fitzgerald, Wolfe, et al., than their mothers and agents put together. These writers, plus many others—though they often fought with Perkins—knew to trust him. So much of our great literature is here in its present form because of him.

May you find your own Maxwell Perkins, or Tony Berg, or Nik Venet. And in the meantime, it might be healthy to take all criticism with a grain, if not a gram, of salt.

7

Straight Lines

*T*HE SHORTEST DISTANCE BETWEEN TWO POINTS is a straight line. Isn't that what we learned in school? And it applies to communication, too. Isn't that what songwriting is? I find that when people communicate in a straight line, it has greater emotional impact on the listener. Would a bullet that ricocheted off someone else hit you as hard? Would you go from L.A. to New York by way of Miami?

By straight lines of communication, of course, I don't mean obvious lines, cliches, or obvious ways of saying things. I mean that when you have something to communicate, musically and/or lyrically, and you put it there in the listener's ear with the precision and power of a laser beam, it will have more impact than if you pitched it out there somewhere in the vicinity of your listener. I call this second, meandering kind of communication "crooked lines." They create vagueness, confusion and, invariably, the listener will tune you out. Just go to an open mic sometimes and watch the audience. They'll listen to the singer for the first few lines and if the melody or lyric has these meandering qualities, the audience gets immediately bored and starts talking amongst themselves.

So what causes their crooked lines of communication? Lack of craft, naturally. But I consider that a catch-all phrase that actually has a lot of causes. I've worked with so many songwriters, I'm amazed at how I can say the very same thing to two of them and they'll hear two entirely different things. One of them—I'll call him the straight writer—will interpret what I say as I mean it and bring back exactly what I ask for. When I critique his work, he gets it and improves his song with every rewrite, learning principles of songwriting as he works on each song. Teaching such a person is a joy. It's as if there's nothing in the way between my words and his mind, between his mind and his actions—the creative process is unencumbered.

Teaching the crooked writer is more of a challenge. He may have the same native intelligence, but there's something in his personality that keeps him from communicating in a straight line. Or even hearing in a straight line. When you tell him something, he'll hear it slightly altered. His chord changes are often arbitrary and his melodies usually lack a sense of inevitability that makes people want to listen to them again and again. His lyrics will be clear to him, because he's familiar with his story, but he'll be unaware that he's not telling it to anyone in a language they can grasp. At best, he will become a competent writer, but he'll never change anyone's life with his songs—not even his own.

I was talking to John Braheny about this and he told me he had consulted with someone who was afraid to write what she really felt for fear her husband would see it and realize how unhappy she was. On the surface, it might seem like this writer's marriage was holding her back. No way! Her fear of communicating was keeping her from using songwriting for one of its best purposes: telling someone what you're uncomfortable telling them face to face. She was losing a golden opportunity!

I won't mention specific situations I have encountered, but I have some of the best writers I have ever heard studying with me. I also teach people who could be great, but something is keeping them from being straight shooters. Either they're doing something in their lives that they feel creepy about, so they're hiding everything—including what they're trying to say in their songs—or they're taking some drug that's altering their personality in some way—the lines get really crooked when that happens. And because I am extremely outspoken about this, we generally decide not to work together once that's revealed. Or, sometimes the person is just afraid. Afraid of change, afraid of rejection. Afraid of life, pretty much. And since communicating is the most dangerous thing going on, they opt not to do it. They go through the motions, but they're not communicating. Not really.

Ironically, the kind of blind spot that burdens the crooked writer is usually so huge, he never thinks about studying with anyone, anyway. He figures he knows it all and stardom is imminent.

The good news is that the process of songwriting itself can begin to reverse the downward spiral in a person's life that's blinding him. Provided he's not too far gone and not chemically altered, he can dig his way out of the hole by communicating honestly about the unhappy marriage, or he can reveal those things about himself he was afraid to look at yesterday. Or he can grieve over the loss of a loved one by sitting down at the piano and letting it pour out.

If this sounds foreign to you, then you've been missing one of the main benefits of our art form. It can relieve a pain of the heart better than any whiskey and it can "shower the people you love with love" better than roses. After a few years of doing it with courage and honesty, your lines will be a lot straighter and your songs will probably be a lot shorter. And so will the distance between you and where you want to be.

8

Reality:
The Training Wheels

*D*ID YOU EVER USE TRAINING WHEELS when you were learning to ride a bicycle? Or did you ever see anyone else use them? The purpose is to keep the bicycle from tipping over. They allow the rider to stay on long enough to perfect some of the skills of riding a bicycle.

Well, I think reality does that for the songwriter. Actually, it does it for any kind of writer. "Write what you know," they tell you in school. And out of school. And "they're" right. Margaret Mitchell only wrote one novel and legend has it, she hid *Gone with the Wind* in coffee cans all over her house, before she showed it to anyone. But she didn't write an action adventure story or a who-done-it set on a European steamer. She wrote what was familiar to her. She may not have lived every scene, but she knew the people. They were composites of people she knew or was related to, in a time and place she understood.

Songwriters who write from a place of truth have the odds in their favor in many ways. First of all, as my mother used to say, "Tell the truth, and you won't have to rely upon your memory."

Reality keeps you from falling off into illogic. Too many of the songs I see from students skip from one thought to another with enough non sequiturs to give you whiplash.

The intention to communicate something real to a real person keeps what you say on track, keeps it flowing logically like a communication you would make. In life, when you're telling someone something that happened or asking that person for something you want, you don't leap from one thought to another or change person or tenses. For that matter, you don't string together cliches and stay on the surface. You say what you mean, interestingly, with pictures and passion. But when a person sits down to write a song, sometimes all of these good habits fall by the wayside. The minute you start "songwriting" instead of communicating, you've blown it. It's like an actor who's "acting." Immediately, the audience is pulled out of the experience of the movie or play and their attention goes on his acting. People should not be conscious that you're writing. And when you're really good at it, they won't be. They'll just be moved. Reality is a way to help you get to that point.

I think of songwriting as a language people speak. When they're just beginning, they can barely speak the language. But after many years, they're fluent. They can pass as a native. So should a person speak on a subject he doesn't know, in a language he doesn't yet speak fluently? How many challenges do we need at one time? And yet day after day, I see people trying to write "save the world" songs—the hardest kind to pull off—when their level of proficiency in the language of songwriting is somewhere around "Where's the bathroom?"

This is another reason why it's such a crucial mistake to chase trends. Based on their desires to get a hit, songwriters sometimes will try to write what someone told them was "happening" rather than what they know about. Of course, there are hundreds of other writers who can write just as well, for whom that subject is real. So the pictures will be real, the logic will be strong and the impact will be superior in their songs. In the trend-chasing songwriter's songs, everything will appear to have been written from the outside at arm's length by someone with very long arms.

Having been a final judge on the "Help Heal L.A." contest, I only heard a small fraction of the entries, but I understand from the preliminary judges that people in Iowa were writing songs about how to solve the problems on the streets of L.A. And of course, on top of their blatant lack of authenticity, they were preaching as well. Strike three.

The final point I'd like to make on the subject of reality in songwriting is, I don't care how popular country music is now. If you really prefer those major seventh chords and cryptic lyrics, please stop writing country songs. Don't you think Nashville can smell your pandering from 2000 miles away? Your style should be based on reality too.

I should acknowledge Nik Venet for some of my viewpoint on this, because when he produced my fourth album, he encouraged me to be who I am, and to write what I know, to be totally truthful as a writer and a performer, as well. I had taken a vacation from artistic integrity and was really enjoying myself writing what I later discovered to be mindless dance music. Now I understand the full meaning of his comment to me when he heard it. "Get real," he said. And so I did.

9

Chimera Is Curable

*N*IK VENET WAS SPEAKING at his ongoing seminar on Creative Record Production for songwriters and performers. He defined the term, "chimera," right out of the dictionary: "a thing of mixed character or fanciful origin, an impossible or foolish fancy . . . in mythology a fire-breathing monster, usually represented as having a lion's head, a goat's body, and a serpent's tail." Chimerical, similarly, was defined as "imaginary, fantastic, unreal . . . absurd, impossible . . . indulging in unrealistic fancies." The realization occurred in all of us at the same moment, I believe. And it was that moment when he reminded us of acts we've seen (and been) where the performance was not a communication with the audience at all; it was merely music that was being sung while the performer watched his or her own fantasies about success, played out on the screen of the mind. This is categorically different from having a dream. I'd like to make that very clear. We all dream and with talent, work and study, we can make dreams a reality. The person who has chimera is not dreaming; he's living in a dream world. And there's a big difference.

Once you know about chimera, you can see it all over the place. Check out the promo pieces you get in the mail from performers. Look at the pictures of themselves they use. Half the time the picture doesn't look anything like the person, and it certainly doesn't represent who the performer really is. At best, it looks like the persona the performer puts on when he/she performs. At worst, it looks like the persona the performer is striving, awkwardly, to impersonate on his way to forgetting who he is, if he ever knew. That's why a songwriter or performer who knows who he is and is willing to communicate it honestly all the way from the promo piece through the performance, is such a refreshing change. And just as human beings are infinitely more interesting than caricatures or cartoons, a real person on stage is more captivating than chimera.

In fact, it's at live performances that chimera can most easily be spotted. In the songs, themselves, it takes the form of poorly crafted "outside-in" songs, I call them. Songs that are written not from the inside, out . . . from a real experience . . . where truth and the emotions naturally born from it can touch someone else in a uniquely individual way. No, "outside-in" songs are written by people on the outside of a situation, or even outside a genre. They've heard folk music and they think it sounds like "this," so they write in a style that's not natural to them because their chimera says they'd be a great folk act. The lyrics come from something they're trying to imitate, rather than from something real. And that's where we find the fire-breathing lion's head, attached to a goat's body with a serpent's tail. The lyrics frequently make no sense and sound like a mishmash of ingredients the writer thinks belong in that style.

Of course, if the act ever sincerely surveyed strangers or bothered to look beyond the row of 10 fans who follow him from show to show, he'd realize the songs make no sense or, at least, have no impact on the listener. You can learn a lot about how much chimera you have going on by watching an impartial audience. If they listen, intently, you're in good shape. If they start talking to each other during your second verse, you need to rework the song from the second verse on. So it's good to stop reading your own fictitious reviews headlining their way across your mind as you sing and observe the audience now and then.

Although chimera is most easily spotted at a live performance, it can be detected in conversation as well. Just talking to someone about his plans in music is a clue. A real artist will discuss his creative challenges, goals and problems. His sights will be on making his work better and his obstacles will be those in his craft. A chimera victim will talk mostly about his "career." His goals will be the degree of success he hopes to achieve, and his obstacles will be viewed as people or politics or "lack of networking opportunities." Such a person gets very upset when you tell him about the major record company which has its fax connected to a shredder. This is the fax number given out for unsolicited promo material.

Chimera is also rampant these days in the studio. One illustration of this is the songwriter who finishes a new song, races into the studio to put it on tape, duplicates it and sends it to everyone he or she has ever run into at any industry event, whether it's requested or not. The note accompanying the submission says the song would be perfect for whatever big name is currently #1 on the charts. In the songwriter's mind, the world is waiting for this new song. Reality lies somewhere South of that. Another studio example of chimera is the writer who's too busy to work on his writing, because he's spending all his time and money in the studio making an artist's demo to send to record companies. Imagine his chagrin when he hears the tiny percentage of acts on the charts who were signed from a tape sent to a record company. But facts rarely deter a chimera victim from his plotted course. First of all, he doesn't hear them. He's too busy listening to the deafening applause in his imagination. And when all submissions are either returned or ignored, he makes the last chimerical stab in the dark: his own independent CD. As Nik Venet explains it, he's now "documenting his mistakes."

The good news is chimera is not that hard to recover from. Once you know what it is, and you're willing to take a long, hard look at your work and your goals and how you plan to get there, it's like waking up from a dream. And it's the truly awake person who can see what's in front of his face. It's the person who's no longer lulled into semi-consciousness by the sound of his own foolish fancies who finds that step by step, he's able to make his dreams come true.

10

Writing from the Inside

"IN HARMONY WITH THE HOMELESS" is a wonderful project developed by Katherine Woodward and Dave Powell. Two professional songwriters team up with members of the Los Angeles Mission to write songs. The experience drove home some important lessons in many areas but, in particular, there were a few principles of good songwriting that were illustrated which I'd like to talk about.

The Mission writers were men and women who had been homeless before coming to the Los Angeles Mission and going through their program of rehabilitation. They were living at the Mission and the songs are to go on a CD, the proceeds of which will benefit the Mission. When Dave Powell was asking me to be a part of it, I asked him about the logistics of the how the songs were written. He mentioned the magic word . . . "journal." The Mission writers keep journals of their experiences. When the professional writers get together with them the first time, the Mission writers read from their journals. It's an extremely inspiring experience, and the process is a living demonstration that reality in songwriting works—and works far better than writing merely based on "an idea."

First, all the pro writers wrote in the musical genre most real and familiar to them, and in which they were the most competent. They didn't switch bags because they thought it was hip or appropriate or marketable. Jan Buckingham co-wrote a country song; Kyle Vincent and I wrote a pop/rock song, Stephen Bray and Alan Sovory wrote an R&B/hip hop tune; Dan Bern co-wrote a folk tune that idiosyncratically wrapped around an askew viewpoint, etc., etc. But it was the lyric approach that was the most telling.

I can only speak of what Kyle and I did with our Mission writer, Joan Foster, but I think everyone worked the same way. She read from her journal. And then we interviewed her. She described what her life was like in vivid, real-life pictures. She was not "writing a song" yet; she was merely communicating. It was deeply moving. It was like a great film with believable acting. We were there, in the middle of it, experiencing it through her words. It wasn't an idea a songwriter got and wrote a song about. It was a slice of real life. Then we took that, found the moment we wanted to capture and we all went to work trying to put it into song form that would heighten the reality and not lose any of it. The melody came from that, and the lyric came from that. We chose the moment of decision when Joan determined to turn her life around. Every picture was something that was actually there that day in the hotel room when she looked at her life and made the decision. The sounds were accurate, as well as the visuals.

Naturally, the pictures you choose and the order you put them in depend upon your craft and experience, but as Jack Webb, playing a detective, used to say in the old "Dragnet" series, "let's start with the facts." If you start with what really happened, in songwriting, you have the power and logic of reality to keep the song on course—like training wheels on a bicycle. You don't fall off into the arbitrary or vague or illogical. The more skilled writer can take these facts to the next level and say something universally true with them. Often, the more specific the pictures, the more universal the message, especially in the hands of a great writer. But even for a beginning writer, starting with something real will give him a tremendous advantage over trying to write a song on the same subject strictly from his imagination.

Allen Roy Scott shared an experience at the end of the day which was also a lesson in songwriting. He said that even though one might expect all the stories to be similar or even the same with so many people speaking of the homeless experience, that each one was unique. He went on to say that's because each individual person is unique, and he has a unique story. I feel this supports the view, again, of writing from what's real. If 30 songwriters all sat at home and wrote a song about the homeless experience, most of them would be making it up from their imagination entirely, and most of the songs would end up saying a lot of the same things. But writing with individual people whose experiences were uniquely theirs, like a finger print or a personality . . . that made for uniquely different songs.

In conclusion, I have observed over and over in songs that move people, that these songs are written from inside the experience, not from outside. Inside is where all the pictures are, all the compelling facts, all the logic and true emotion. Everything else is just guesswork. Even when a writer hasn't technically lived every word, he's drawing from a truth he does have first-hand experience about, sometimes dressed up in other characters. But outside-in writing strictly from the imagination or "a good idea" is to the true art of songwriting what paint-by-number "mallards in flight" is to an inspired oil painting by a master. The former will have, at best, some short-lived popularity, whereas the latter can expand and enrich the listener and live through time, being rediscovered by new generations who may wear different fashions in clothing and musical feel, but share a common humanity. Melody and lyric with truth will touch that humanity forever.

11

Songwriters Say It All

S ONGWRITERS REVEAL SO MUCH about themselves, perhaps it's a
blessing that the ones who reveal unpleasant things are
usually oblivious to it. The very qualities that help make a great
writer—powers of observation, interest in something outside him/
herself, ability to feel, willingness to reveal and communicate, and
facility with the language of words and music—these qualities
usually come across in the songs, making the songwriter seem
attractive and likable, someone you would want to know.

The qualities often found in a person you wouldn't naturally
be drawn to are the same characteristics that cripple his work as a
songwriter—unconsciousness of anything outside himself, insen-
sitivity to the details of life, being cut off from his own emotions
and an unwillingness to let others actually see who he is, plus an
ineptness with the tools of communication. The catch 22 is that a
person like this will reveal all these attributes without knowing it,
because his powers of perception and communication are limited
to begin with. He or she will rail at a lover or parent or friend for all
those dreadful things that we may believe or understand actually
happened, but we rarely come away enlightened from it. And
without the understanding and wisdom a great writer would add
to the same song, the "unattractive" writer just looks like a victim
or a nag. Even though his intention was to get us to agree about the

lover, we seldom dislike the lover as much as the writer in those instances.

I have been in the audience when some of my students have performed, and I have seen the effect of well-crafted revelation. Steve Wagner writes:

"She asks him 'how was your day'
And he answers 'okay'
but he doesn't give any details.
And it never occurs to him
To ask about hers
'Cause he's too busy reading the mail.
He rises once to kiss her
But all he really gives her
Is an intimate clue
That only one of the two is in love."

This plot in less skillful hands could be (and has been) a disaster, but Steve's song develops beautifully giving true insight into the pain felt by both sides when one loves but is not in love with his partner. The melody is also hauntingly powerful, and I have seen a roomful of noisy people quiet down by the end of the first verse.

Jim Dean, a recognizable actor who, I predict, will soon be a recognized songwriter, sets his song ("The Last Supper") at a restaurant as he and the woman he still loves find it impossible to talk to each other in any meaningful way:

"You pull your angel hair
I stab my Caesar
I'll always have your smile
Taped to my freezer."

As he unravels his story in pictures, we discover his wit, his vulnerability, his loyalty and, perhaps, his Achilles heel. At the end of the song, we like him. He's human. We can see ourselves in there. There's room for us—not in the gaping holes of logic that so often occur in songs—but in the specific pictures that look familiar to us. Len Brunson (w/Richard White) wrote a song so vividly depicting a specific woman as such bad news, we all feel we either know her or are her by the end of the song. He isn't complaining about "women," he's describing one particular woman. He sets it to a gorgeous, dark, classic jazz-blues melody:

"She's a hopeless situation
In her tight silk dress
She's a needless complication
She's a heartbreak at best
And if you wanna find her
Put on your walking shoes
She's just around the corner from the blues."

In the last verse, he takes responsibility for getting himself into this fine mess, becoming a three dimensional character, himself, and therefore even more likable.

"A fool with both his eyes closed
He could've read the signs
But I did what I always do
Temptation made me blind
Now she's left me here with nothing
And nothing left to lose
Just around the corner from the blues."

Cheryl Foster has grown so much as a writer in the past year, not only in craft, but in the courage to reveal. This song would have to be heard in its entirety to show her courage for revelation, but her first verse illustrates the point about powers of observation and how interesting someone can be when they're interested:

"I keep some clownfish in my aquarium
And I watch them swimming every day
I keep them safe from harm
In my tropical display
And I can see my own face reflecting off
The glass and in their black eyes
I can sense they're really bored
And I can sympathize."

Naturally, I've given examples of good writing where the songwriter reveals truthful, human situations and qualities which attract us to him or her. At open mike nights, you will see the full spectrum. You will hear the other kind of writers, the oblivious, self-centered kind, but you probably won't meet them. You'll be too busy talking to the charismatic one who is genuinely interested in you.

12

Art and Romance:
An Analogy

YOU HAVE TO UNDERSTAND I just returned from Cannes, where Midem and mayhem were flying as fast and furiously as hormones and hip hop. Midem, as you probably know, is the humongous International Music Industry Convergence that occurs annually in Southern France and is attended by about 10,000 people. In the old days, I understand, foreign record labels and subpublishers listened over headsets to products and wrote checks and signed contracts on the spot, on a regular basis. Now it's a bit different. You have 10 to 30-minute appointments with various companies from differing countries, which have been set up in advance for either minutes, days or months. And it helps, immensely, to be referred by someone they know. Most of the meaningful meetings take place outside of the Palais, or convention hall, at one of the palatial hotels on the main strip. Between the hours of 1AM to 4AM, there is schmoozing that makes Los Angeles look like a sleepy hick town. But how much of that actually pays off is for someone else to tell me. I had too serious a case of jet lag to go to the Martinez Hotel Bar for even one night.

What I did observe, though, is an analogy that's been building in my head since I got home. It's the analogy between art and romance. Most people have been dating longer than they've been writing songs, with the possible exception of the painfully shy and the wildly precocious. So think back to those times which linger in your memory as the sweetest . . . those romances or that one romance in which your heart was deeply involved. How did you act? When you talked to her/him, you were really interested in the conversation. You didn't feel like you were off watching yourself from a distance, wondering how you were doing and wondering if it was working the magic you needed to get the results you wanted. That's seduction, not romance. Now apply that to songwriting. When you're really interested in saying something, musically and lyrically . . . when you have something to communicate because your heart is so full of an emotion or a realization that it simply spills out . . . that's when you make real contact. That's when your listeners are moved, your audience gets to know you, other singers want to sing your songs.

Obviously, you have to know how to write songs first. But assuming you have control of the craft and have honed it to such an extent that you can are fluently conversant in the language of songwriting, that's when you can consciously decide how to communicate. Do you try to dazzle your listeners with how clever you are drawing attention to the frame rather than the picture? Will you write any way you think will please someone, whether it's your natural style or not? Like the Valley Girl who tries to write rap because it's "happening?" Will you take on a viewpoint that's not yours or speak a way that's not natural to you in order to achieve some imagined desired result? Like the Cape Cod yuppie who parachutes in on Nashville because he hears Garth is "looking." Have you ever been out with someone who's trying to order dinner in a foreign language he/she doesn't speak, or discuss wines they know nothing about? It all looks pretty similar to me.

Do you say what you think they want to hear, in a drum groove, a bass line or a lyric? Or do you simply translate your own individual viewpoint into song form, holding onto the integrity of being yourself every step of the way? Once you do this, and do it honestly and superbly, you must understand that those who don't want your songs are simply not your target audience. Just like the analogy of romance. If you're really being yourself and your dinner partner doesn't want to see you again, you're with the wrong partner. Wouldn't you rather know that now than pretend to be some way you're not and have to be that way for the rest of the relationship? It reminds me of the band whose music is really outside, lyrically they're somewhere between Dylan and bomb throwing leftists and the label wants them to do "this one Diane Warren song" so that they can get widespread crossover airplay, etc., etc. Of course, the fans who buy the album based on the single are horrified by the rest of the album and they end up being one of many flash-in-the-pan bands whose options get dropped. Ah, the heartbreak of the one-night-stand.

At Midem, it seems that the people who were the most successful were the ones who genuinely care about the people they contact there. Relationships are begun and nurtured over years between publishers and subpublishers, between record companies and publishers and recording artists. But people who came looking for a quick deal or immediate funds were usually disappointed. It's a people event. You have to get to know people and have their best interests in mind as well as your own. After all, it's not just Americans there. And, therefore, it's not just attorneys representing talent. Companies want to know the people they're doing business with, the track record, the potential, the plans. Slam-bam, thank you ma'am, doesn't make it in the Midem big business arena anymore. I witnessed some very sweet long term publisher relationships. Watching the lovely and graceful Molly Hyman deal with her subpublishers, I felt I was at a family reunion, rather than at a business meeting. Once again, sincere communication succeeded over manipulative conversation. Those who were comfortable with themselves and genuinely interested in others did way better than those who had that desperate look of 2AM in a singles bar. As Nik Venet says, "Everybody writes. Everybody sings. Not everybody tells the truth. And it's the truth that touches people." In art and apparently, sometimes in business too. And wherever I saw these successful intercontinental interactions, I always felt I was witnessing a romance, never a seduction. But, then, I never made it to the Martinez.

13

Do You Read?

WHEN CHAUNCEY GARDENER in *Being There* says "I don't read," all the party guests agree that no one reads, no one has the time. And the audience laughs. Of course Chauncey means he simply doesn't know how to read. So that's his excuse.

My excuse used to be that I couldn't afford it. Time was money and since I pored over every word as if it were poetry, even the novels, I simply couldn't take the time to do it. Something had to be work-related in order for me to allow myself to do it. But my entire approach to work and writing changed when I met Nik Venet, as my album producer and mentor. I won't go so far as to say I read merely for pleasure, now, because I'm still too work-motivated to simply engage in something as frivolous as pleasure on a regular basis. But I will say I am armed with all the reasons necessary for me to allow myself to read regularly, and I thought you might need some and, therefore, benefit from hearing some of mine.

"How can you write if you don't read?" asks Nik Venet at the beginning of his ongoing Songwriting/Performance seminar series. Everyone is handed a reading list when they first arrive. The writers listed are all amazing novelists and poets whom Venet has discovered around two to fifteen years before the world at large does. Both Toni Morrison and Rita Dove won prestigious new writer awards two years after their names appeared on the Venet reading list. So it's like being the first on your block to discover these exquisite writers in many cases. And since I coordinate and host the seminar, I can't be the only one not reading these writers, so that's one work-related rationale for having to do something so pleasurable. I eased into it with Toni Morrison's *Jazz* on tape read by the author. It was totally enthralling, and her control over the language so masterful and inspiring, I found myself traveling long distances at the slightest provocation, just to be in the car where I could put the tape in my stereo. Since I was doing two things at once, I could easily justify spending the time on it.

I can't remember the exact order of discovery, but all of the authors offered a different type of treasury. Bukowski's world might seem on the surface like it had nothing in common with the likes of me, a Dallas-born Doctor's daughter. And yet the irony with which he draws characters and writes about relationships hits a common chord with anyone who's ever really lived, whatever the neighborhood they may have lived in. Lyle Lovett has a wonderful command of that kind of irony in a songwriting genre. Whether he ever read Bukowski, I don't know. But what I like in one, I also appreciate in the other. Raymond Carver's *Short Cuts* was on the list two years before Robert Altman attempted to turn it into a film. It took me until the fourth story to stop waiting "for something to happen" and start grasping the power in his detailed reality.

Some people read to get ideas for songs. That's not how it works for me. There's so much more depth an author can provide in the long form of a novel, that the fleshed out real people characters and the intricacies of the plots involve us in a way that seems to give texture to our own writing of songs. It's a little like "back story" in screen writing—the rest of the story of the characters that is not shown on the screen, but which fills out the characters somehow just because the screenwriter knows it.

Singer/songwriter Corwyn Travers explains it like this, "Literature is a compatible art form, not a competitive one, so it's easier to learn from it. Furthermore, a book is limitless in what it can give . . . including putting a visual to our own feelings." I happen to know Corwyn was reading Dorothy Allison's *Bastard Out of Carolina*, one of my personal favorites from the list, while she was writing a particular song as a seminar assignment. She was inspired to write the last line of the following, autobiographical verse by her intense experience of reading the book: "Father spent his days behind the wheel/Told me I would never miss a meal/But hunger was a part of me/And it rocked me every night to sleep."

Monique Dayan loved Joan Didion's use of language in *Slouching Towards Bethlehem* and *The White Album*. And in reading *Jazz*, Monique said she would spend ten minutes on one paragraph just to get the depth of what Toni Morrison was saying. I did the same thing, but with my rewind button in the car. I remember when I first started reading *Cowboys Are My Weakness*, a group of stories by Pam Houston, I kept wondering if she was a songwriter as well. Every other line sounded like a lyric, packed with rich analogies and imagery.

The *L.A. Times* in an article March 7, quotes Neil Postman's book, *Amusing Ourselves to Death* (Viking Penguin, 1986) "By not reading," the article says, "we lose 'a sort of psychic habit, a logic, a sense of complexity, an ability to spot contradictions and even falsity.'" The book deals with the wide ramifications of reading's decline on a society. And in a culture where sound bytes provide the news and people's attention span can only last four minutes when MTV is flashing simultaneous non-sequitur images on the screen, it's no wonder that beginning songwriters have so much trouble writing a clear, meaningful, logical lyric. How can someone develop the foresight for chess when they've been raised exclusively on Pac-Man?

Well, I just finished *Waiting To Exhale* last night. And Terry McMillan took me on an engrossing journey into the lives of four fascinating women. (It was on the Venet list a year before it was announced that a movie will be made of it, starring Whitney Houston.) The characters each had a uniquely different voice and viewpoint and McMillan remained true to each one throughout. Little clues planted in the beginning blossomed later and even though some reviewers will probably think it was tied up with a bow at the end, I liked that facet of it.

So now I'm reading for pleasure, for inspiration, for the vicarious thrill of all those other lives, for the texture it gives my own life and, therefore my work. And I'm also enjoying being in a community of other songwriters who are reading the same novels and poems. Of course, a reader could get whip lash jumping from Raymond Chandler to Terry McMillan in the same night. But while we're recuperating, we could curl up with a really good book.

14

Cookies or Newspapers?

PRODUCERS, TEACHERS, PUBLISHERS AND MANAGERS aren't the only people giving feedback to songwriters. Every time you collaborate or hear a friend's song, you are in the position to give your feelings on a song or portions of it. How you do that could be very important to the person listening, to your relationship with him/her in the future, even to his/her future writing.

Have you ever seen a dog trainer working to get a dog to learn something? The dog rolls over and the trainer gives him a dog biscuit or cookie. Have you ever seen a dog owner trying to train his dog by tapping or hitting him on the head with the newspaper? The dog gets some message, but rarely does he get the right one. He may start to lower his head when he passes his owner. But the dog doesn't remember what he did right, compare it to what he did to incur the rolled up newspaper punishment, and vow to change his behavior. Dogs don't think in such intricate complexities.

All the dog knows is it's not safe in there. It reminds me of the Gary Larson cartoon where the dog owner is talking up a storm to his dog, and the dog only hears "blah, blah, blah, Ginger, blah, blah, blah."

Of course, people are reputed to be smarter than dogs, so if we're criticized or ridiculed or shamed, we have the intelligence to realize what the newspaper pat means. Or are we? The creative spirit is a delicate thing, if not fragile. I've seen it banished with a careless word, not to come out of hiding for years. The best-meaning mentors and friends and collaborators can do more damage than good by what they consider constructive criticism. How the message is delivered is extremely important, especially during the years before a writer has certainty in his/her craft and artistic viewpoint, even style.

Of course, there are those writers who are either successfully or unsuccessfully pulling the wool over lots of people's eyes, including their own. These people are trying to slide by with not much to say, breaking no new ground, and writing rehashes of everything they've ever heard. With writers like this, it's really tempting to just bust them, if for no other reason than to let them know we're in on their secret. We know they're trying to con us, and we know they're skating on the surface. The only problem with busting them is that what we don't know is if there's anything worth plumbing beneath the surface. Nothing makes someone feel more helpless than to feel the rug of mediocrity being pulled out from under him/her to reveal there's no floor, much less a basement. The chances are he's been writing that way because he's afraid to look. You have to invite and inspire him to go there, not force him.

Being a cat person, rather than a dog owner, and knowing that cats are pretty hard to train, I mentioned my dog training analogy to my producer, Nik Venet. He has a theory that training and obedience is only the first level. The truly well trained dogs are not those who simply do tricks or act nice to get a reward or avoid punishment. When you see a dog that has moved to the level with his owner or trainer of trust and mutual obligation, you really have teamwork. I liked this analogy for songwriters. Whomever you're showing your songs to, or whoever is getting feedback from you on their songs, trust and mutual obligation is the atmosphere you want to establish. As I look back on some of my earlier publishing deals, I see more of a newspaper and cookie analogy. Now, when I write a new song, I trust my publisher will understand what I'm trying to accomplish and give me feedback, if necessary, to help me get there. It won't be like I'm on an alien planet trying to make contact with someone who speaks another language. And because we're in business together, I feel an obligation to give him songs on a certain level, and I trust myself to do it.

When I give feedback to students, I try to come from a place of trust and mutual obligation. After all, they're paying me to tell them the truth, as I see it, in a way that will make them better writers, not make them want to quit writing. And I find the best way to do this is to find what is strong about the song and in their viewpoint and approach, and then point out any place in the song (lyrically, melodically, harmonically or rhythmically) that keeps it from remaining at that highest level. I'm frequently teased by those who take a harsher approach. I'm said to be able to see any cup as half full, even when there's only a drop of water in it. But to quote Nik Venet, "The mind cannot image a non-occurrence," so why concentrate on what's not there? Let's take a look at what is present and build on it.

Sometimes when people are being criticized, the critic simply is not well-read or well-listened enough to grasp what the writer is going for. A publisher, teacher or collaborator's musical orientation can frequently render him outside the frame of reference of the person showing him something. And lyrically, there may be an allusion to something he hasn't read or heard of that the target audience would understand, so if he criticizes it saying "no one would get that," he reveals more of his own shortcomings than those of the writer.

Publishers have traditionally had the unpopular task of saying to a writer, "You're 'out there,' pal, let's reel you in." Ironically, though, it's the out-thereness that frequently sets a writer above the crowd and makes people stop and listen. I keep a Nik Venet quote on my piano:

"The important thing for a songwriter is not to write songs that songwriters are doing already, a little better or a little worse; but to write those songs that at present are not being written."

And once you get that song, or the concept for that song, remember to show it to someone with whom you have trust and mutual obligation. And when you hear someone else's song or song idea, remember to create an environment of safety. Knowing full well that outside our window, there's a music business jungle, we don't also need to have snakes and charging rhinos inside our music rooms. Let's unroll the newspapers and either read them or put them at the bottom of the bird cage.

15

The New Literacy

THEY'RE ADVERTISING BOOKS ON TELEVISION. Have you ever seen those commercials that talk about a story, trick you into thinking it's all about your life, and then spring it on you that it's a classic novel or play? They're great. Recently I also read about a new PBS TV show advertised which will put a dog character, "Wishbone," running through all the great books to introduce them to children. Whitney Houston is starring in a film version of *Waiting to Exhale,* a literate, realistic, down-to-earth novel by Terry McMillan, which Houston bought the rights to and is currently filming.

So literacy is becoming hip. Whoda thunk it? Well, for one, Nik Venet has been known to predict the future (especially in the careers of the artists he broke as a producer—Ronstadt, Beach Boys, Jim Croce, John Stewart, Lou Rawls, Dory Previn, Fred Neil, to name a few) so when he predicted a new wave of literacy, we listened. In fact, *Waiting to Exhale* was on his reading list over two years ago. Four years ago, he predicted the coffee house upsurge and the new "folk" scene, although his definition of folk is a little wider than some people's. When he started handing out reading lists and telling people if they don't read, they can't write, people left the seminar by the droves. But more came to take their places. And a dozen of the ones who stayed, three years later, became what's known as "The Campfire Conspiracy." These songwriter/ singers have been working diligently on the craft of songwriting, never settling for an okay line when a great one was possible, never allowing a mere serviceable melody to slip in when a killer melody was just around the corner.

With only one instrument and voice, each of these songwriters has been standing in front of huge auditoriums of high school students, some of whom look like they're at the assembly against their wills, that they're much too hip to sit there and listen. So these particular students talk non-stop during the setting up and the introduction of the Campfire Conspiracy as an official GRAMMY in the Schools® Outreach Program, put on by NARAS (National Academy of Recording Arts & Sciences). But a funny thing happens once the songs begin. You can see this strange thing take shape in the faces of the high school students. It's called interest.

They poke each other when Sara Kim Wilde sings:

"Sitting at the Kmart Counter
Wishing I had more mustard
And more money
And more time."

When Steve Wagner sings, "It's just something you do when only one of the two is in love," there's a look of recognition on the faces of kids who look too young to have had a relationship at all, much less a failed one. But of course, it's high school, and we all remember how intense it felt. We remind them of things, and they remind us. All the performers sit on stage looking out at the audience as everyone sings, one at a time. So we're actually both getting a show. Who's to say the one the students are seeing is any better than the one they're being?

Corwyn Travers introduces her song by saying her husband is the one man who wouldn't let her push him away, and Michelle Fox sings of that first encounter between you, the man you loved, and his new girlfriend. At a high school in Manhattan Beach, two girls on the second row start crying when Marc Corwin Bruce sings his song called "Fathers in the Park" about single father weekends. I've heard a lot of songs on this subject, but this is not just another one. This is decidedly different from singing at an open mic, in front of fifty other songwriters. These are the record buyers—they aren't trained to applaud for their friends in order to get applause when they get up to sing. This is a tough, unforgiving crowd with a short attention span.

Steve Jackson Wilde and Jim Dean are recognizable actors, as well as being excellent songwriters, so there's usually a whisper around the room when their credits are mentioned. Someone has either seen Steve in a movie or recognized Jim as the Wendy's hamburger or Eggo guy. After all, when you're in the living room of a high school student via the almighty television, you have arrived. Luckily their songs are mesmerizing, or there would be some very disappointed teenagers out there. Can't allow their heroes to let them down.

Leslie Claussen sings,

"A child wanders next to me,
Then backs away mistrustfully,
'Cause I'm the stranger,
I could be the danger
Lurking in the dark.
It breaks my heart,
And it's strange the way
This city holds so many people
So far apart."

Combined with the darkness of the melody and guitar, the lyric reminds them of a truth they know too well. Oddly, we feel less isolated when we hear isolation described so truthfully and with so much insight.

The press has been amazing and each picture always contains Bill Berry. His song, "The Brick" invariably draws tremendous attention.

> "A brick can start a riot,
> Throw it from an angry mob.
> I've seen people use it for a pillow,
> Simply 'cause they lost their job.
> Build a cellar full of noise
> Or a cellar for your wine;
> Wrap it in a pretty package,
> Sell a Pet Brick you can buy.
> Drop one off a building,
> Play a game of brick roulette
> Or try doing something useful,
> Maybe build a laundromat.
> If you're hiding from the IRS,
> Use a brick to jam the door.
> Yeah, you can tell a lot about a man
> By what he uses his brick for."

Bill lists a litany of uses for a brick until the metaphor is driven home—in a Mercedes. Even the most jaded, insistently uninterested of high school students cannot resist this one.

Each performer is introduced by Nik Venet, who gives a pearl of songwriting/literary/artistic wisdom which the song illustrates. The show ends with my singing "Rosebud," the title song of the album I'm currently recording, which Venet is producing. Even though *Citizen Kane* is not "literature," it's part of our literary frame of reference. Great films, great books and great songs all comprise the new literacy. And when you've looked into the faces of the new generation day after day, you begin to believe Venet was right. Triple A and Americana formats are not just for baby boomers. Substance is in demand at every age group.

"How in the world do you get them to listen like that?" asks one of the teachers at Van Nuys High School. I think to myself, "We just give them something to listen to."

16

Burning Desire to Communicate

I'VE BEEN WORKING WITH STEVE SCHALCHLIN, recently, on an amazing show he's writing (with Jim Brochu) called "The Last Session," about Steve's own struggle with AIDS. I have always told my students they should have a "burning desire to communicate" something, before they start writing, and this advice is exemplified in Steve's recent work, perhaps better than I've ever seen it. Steve is writing what he's experienced, what he feels and what he has a burning desire for people to know—that they should value every moment of their lives, among other things. He communicates this by telling his own personal truth, with such a sense of irony and wisdom, that the specific begins to touch that universal nerve. At the bottom of his email messages it says, "Steve Schalchlin is in the bonus round." After two serious bouts with HIV related illnesses, he describes this holiday season as the second Christmas he wasn't supposed to be around for. He's not only around; he's writing some of the best songs I've heard.

Most songwriters in Los Angeles know Steve from his many tireless years helping songwriters and fighting for songwriters' rights at the National Academy of Songwriters. During that time, I always acknowledged him for his wonderful work in this area, but I would always end my discussions with a reminder to him that he was also a songwriter. One time, I even lured him into taking my class so he'd have a songwriting deadline every week—and he did write some good songs then. But now, by his own admission, he has connected his skill with his deep intention to communicate something, to reveal something and to illuminate. The result is a group of songs that knocked out the few people he has shown them to: John Bettis, Marie Cain, Alan O'Day, and me, among others. When he finally begins performing these songs publicly, it will amaze everyone. (He's been invited to debut the work in progress at the January meeting of the group, "Wine, Women and Song" and he performed one of the songs at the recent Los Angeles Women In Music Soiree to great response.) Steve had already developed the craft of songwriting from many years of work. What he has added to it recently is the fire.

"I respect honest, articulate expressions of the heart. It either 'grows corn or it don't.'" (Steve is a fellow Texan.) He goes on, "If I hear a real person who's alive and thinking underneath that horrible demo, I'm going to search deeper and see what this person is capable of, but you can't give a person something to say. People either have something to say or they don't. This means they must be alive and attentive. And not just to the rest of the world, but to each other, too. To each other, sometimes, most of all." Steve is Creative Consultant for Kim and Ronda Espy at Bob-A-Lew Music.

It's so interesting to talk to people I respect and hear them all say the same thing, and it's especially gratifying when it corroborates what I've been thinking and saying, of course. But I heard the wonderful David Wilcox last week, in concert. And he said, in introducing a song, that he writes from little realizations. I couldn't agree more. Nik Venet is constantly asking for a realization or a win in a song, when he's listening. And he's created a group of songwriters who are taking that message home every

week to thousands of high school students for whom they perform—not an easy audience. As Steve Schalchlin went on to say,
"It's our job to lift mankind into a higher state of living. The
songwriter must accept the responsibility that he must think and
feel and appreciate and observe and then find the truth in these
things and write about them." (Echoes of Nik Venet's mantra
about "Starting from a sentence of truth" and his prodding to
"keep a journal, learn to observe people and find the remarkable
in the everyday."

I have students who don't realize they have something to say
until I ask them certain questions. They look for the answers and
discover they have something to say. They never thought to write
a song about that, but that is where their song is. It is in the fire of
their burning desire to communicate. You can tell by talking to
someone if s/he has a particular viewpoint. Think of the people
you know who enlighten you by talking to them. They are the
ones who think like writers. Perhaps they are writers. To quote
Steve again, "The problem for most writers is they have nothing to
say—period. If you do not know why you are writing a song, the
audience will not know why you wrote it either. And they won't
care."

Performing with the Campfire Conspiracy in the GRAMMY in
the Schools® project has made me realize how impactful a unique
viewpoint is. When Robert Thornburg sings "Superbowl Sunday"
about a little girl in a dumpster, her brother, her grandmother and
a head of lettuce, the students are seeing a slice of life cut with a
unique knife. And the same can be said of every single performer.
But they don't write that way to be different or unique. They write
that way because each one person IS unique and s/he is writing
from a unique, personal viewpoint on a subject where there's a
burning desire to say something.

When I witness the urgency with which Steve Schalchlin is
creating the best work of his life, and the honesty and courage he
is employing to write it, I have less and less patience with people
who try to manipulate the market to get a hit. It rarely works and

when it does, it doesn't last. It's a waste of energy and talent, not to mention that valuable commodity, time. "The Last Session" is rekindling my belief in the fire of honest, direct and powerful communication—in songs and in life.

17

Some Points to View on Viewpoints

I'M SURE YOU'VE FELT IT. That tingling you get right before a really great idea comes, sort of like the way you feel at the roulette table—for you gamblers—when you know your color or number is coming up. There are other more pertinent analogies, but I'll leave them to your imagination.

So how do you get these ideas? It's so hard to answer that with a straight face. People ask me all the time, "How did you think of that?" What I actually want to say is: "Here's what you do. You live as ethical and courageous a life as you possibly can for fifteen years, writing songs all the while, and spending a lot of time making sure you work very hard to keep your creative spirit alive as well as your desire to communicate. Then you go over to a relatively comfortable chair and start writing." That's the truthful answer. But that's not what people want to hear. So, I'll see if I can give you some tips on the craft or some shortcuts.

In all fairness to the shortcut theory, I have developed a series of exercises which work incredibly well on writers who already have something to say. I can help people get out the good concepts, effortlessly, and put them into song form one step at a time, so that it flows naturally rather than being a grind. And after every 8-week semester, I'm told that it works very well. What is more difficult is giving someone the desire and ability to say something worth saying. And since this is FAR MORE IMPORTANT than HOW you say it, I guess the axiom is true that writers are born or evolved into and not made or taught. At least I believe it to be so.

So let's assume you already have something to say, that you're a born writer. How can you get better at this thing? Well, before I get to the craft part, let me suggest some very un-Hollywood traits you might want to develop. Become really interested in people. And really listen to what they have to say. Especially when they're speaking honestly from their hearts. And if you can't get them to, ask them questions that will get them to. My high-school reunion class hates to see me coming. Because every reunion, I put everyone in a big circle and ask probing questions. Not about what work they had last week, but about how they really feel about life and themselves and their loved ones, you know, the real stuff. And after I'm gone, they're all really glad to have had an opportunity to talk about it—and I have inspiration for lots of songs.

In spite of what I just said about getting ideas from other people's experience, I believe the song is best written from our own viewpoint. That way, it all rings true, and it comes out from a real center and hangs together on a logical thread. I know that's a far-fetched theory and quite a controversial one for those "crafties" out there who think it's all done in the imagination. Well, maybe my definition of imagination is different. Certainly you use the imagination, but simply as a vehicle to transport your viewpoint.

In movie assignment writing, I have to transport my viewpoint all the time. One day I've assumed the viewpoint of a naive male black virgin from the ghetto who's studying karate with an Eastern guru and has just fallen in love for the first time—with Vanity (*The Last Dragon*—song: "First Time On A Ferris Wheel"). The next assignment, I'm a red-haired, self-sufficient female 10-year-old who lives alone with her horse and monkey (*The New*

Adventures of Pippi Longstocking). I didn't write those from the outside, "imagining" what they would say. I assumed the viewpoint, became those characters and looked at the world through their eyes.

Shakespeare supposedly never left his home town. Of course, my father read a very convincing argument that all of Shakespeare's works were written by Queen Elizabeth. The author of this outlandish premise argued that Shakespeare lacked the "experience" to write what he did. Well, without getting too mystical, let me just say that I feel our experience is much vaster than would appear by reviewing those actions we can immediately remember. So when people say they get ideas for songs from the newspaper, or from a book or conversation, I say fine. But I would suggest, if you do this, that you get inside the lyric by assuming the viewpoint of the person who is speaking in the song. Otherwise, you miss half the joy of writing in the first place—being able to expand who you are into other viewpoints and personalities. It's like a vacation. Why miss it?

So here is an exercise you can do to limber up your ability to shift viewpoints. This is not from my 8-week courses, because those exercises are confidential. But I've used this at seminars, and it's fun. Select a movie you love, and write titles from the viewpoint of all the main characters. For instance, in *Gone with the Wind*, Scarlett's view of life and relationships was quite different from Melanie's. And theirs were different still from Ashley Wilkes' and Rhett Butler's, which were also pivotally different from each other. Once you get the title, think through your story, being that character. Look at how you interrelate with the other characters. Basically, all this is doing for you is tapping some set of emotions you might not have felt at the moment. A more contemporary movie might be more relevant for you; I used this one because it's so universally known.

Writing from your own viewpoint as an artist is rewarding but can be tricky. When your first album comes out, people try to peg you so they'll know what to expect next time. Of course, as an artist, you can have many viewpoints because as a person, you can. Joni Mitchell has changed and evolved over the years, musically and lyrically, as a prime example of how an artist needs and wants to grow and change. Rod Stewart has also changed quite a lot since he began. The public, though, if you're not careful, will typecast you from what they think your viewpoint is—or from the viewpoint of yours with which they once agreed—and when you veer from that, they can get upset. It's like the plight of an actor who gets associated with one particular part and the audiences won't accept him playing any other type of character. For this reason, a lot of artists also write for and produce other artists (Prince, Jimmy Jam & Terry Lewis vs. their band The Time). This way, you can be everyone you really are—in all the musical styles and with all the viewpoints—and still do your own artist thing, retaining narrower parameters of what you want to say.

Part II

Clarity

18

Truth vs. Facts in Songwriting

"JUST GIVE ME THE FACTS, MA'AM," Sergeant Friday used to say in Dragnet. And somehow we got the idea that the facts and the truth were synonymous. And frequently they are. But in songwriting, confusing the facts with the truth is like mistaking clay for sculpture. What is done with the facts, and which facts are chosen—that's everything.

First of all, let's be clear on what kind of songwriting is being discussed here. I'm not talking about "formula" stock songwriting. I'm talking about songs that are written from a desire to say something. Songs that communicate some truth always have a longevity beyond mere "hit" songs, because that truth lives beyond fashion. Though the production style on the first record may become obsolete, the message in the lyric and melody will not. So the children of the fans who first heard it will discover it again in the modern clothing of new arrangement and production later on. That's what makes a classic, a standard.

Let's take a very down-to-earth example. You're writing a song for your parents' anniversary. You want to express the truth that they are heroes to you, that their love has withstood more than many others could have survived and they are deserving of the prize that comes with such courage and constancy—whatever you deem that to be. Now imagine that story told with these facts: You remember when you were six years old, he came home at 3 in the morning and she screamed her head off and threw a mirror at him. Seven years of bad luck later, they took you to Disneyland where you got really sick on those greasy cinnamon things. Lest you think I am jesting, let me assure you I've heard songs that have more inappropriate facts in them than this. And when I question their presence in the song, I hear the defense, "Well, that's what happened." Yes, I'm sure it did. But the sun came up again this morning and it doesn't go in every song you write.

Deciding which facts to use is what separates a true storyteller from a poser/lyric writer. One of the four qualities that makes a great songwriter, according to my mentor, Nik Venet, is "the talent to communicate truth and conceive from scratch realistic characters and situations in order to do so." Of course, many of these characters and situations will be straight from your life; many of them will be composites from different times and places in your life. But arranging those facts, shaping them into the story that will tell the truth you're imparting is like a sculptor taking a hunk of clay and bending it, adding a glob here and a twist there, taking part of it away.

When Paul Gallico (The Snow Goose) was asked what the hardest part of writing was, he said "the part you leave out." When you think about it, any situation you're writing about is so full of information, you have to be able to look at it as you would one of those "3 D" pictures and see the picture inside it. You have to look at life, full of irrelevant, fascinatingly distracting facts, strip them away and find the few key elements with which to tell your story, your truth. And if you tell it specifically, honestly, remarkably enough, other people will see their own truth in it. People will relate to it whose facts are totally different from yours. Truth is shared by many, specific facts are not.

Have you ever noticed two children from the same family remember the past totally differently? They may have had the same parents, lived in the same household, and yet they have totally different viewpoints and personalities. The facts surrounding them were the same, but they saw them differently, reacted differently to them. So to find any two people who actually share the same, objective experience is very difficult. It's better to paint with pictures the listener can put himself into. You'll never find the exact experience he had. That's why facts that don't go to the next level of revealing some truth are so lame in a song. A long time ago, of course, they used to sing songs to tell the news— before the days of newspapers. Bards would go from town to town singing of politics, the latest scandal, and other Hardcopy type lyrics.

But art has always bent objective reality a bit to make its point. Novelists and playwrights are constantly using conglomerates of people they know for characters. And many visual artists, after they've mastered the craft of realism move into a less photo-graphic style to express their feelings about the subject. Matisse is said to have had a visitor in his art studio one time, an artist's worst nightmare, a person who avowedly doesn't "know anything about art" but knows what he likes. He pointed to a canvas of Matisse's and said to the artist, "That woman's arm is too long." Matisse answered, "That is not a woman, sir, it's a painting."

Today, especially with the renewed literacy in all art, songs, poems, novels, plays, films, and short stories are expected to lead the listener/reader into a world so fascinating and so real, that he discovers real people there, some of whom are himself. And by being all those people, he can shift his viewpoint and know what it feels like to be other people and to feel what they feel. You, as a songwriter, will have helped him achieve this. And not by sticking to the facts, ma'am, but by sculpting them into the truth.

19

When Little Things
Mean a Lot

*N*OT KNOWING THAT SPACE HAD BEEN SAVED for this article, I
hadn't come up with one. About five minutes before my
class started, I found out I was invited to write one. So I asked my
students what they thought would be a good subject.

"Think of something people need to know" I called inno-
cently, from the kitchen, as the class started sitting around the
dining room table. "What do women want?" answered Steve
Wagner, one of my more droll students. Then Mike Booth suggested I write about all the things I mention in passing to my
students, but which are considered by many people to be unimportant, or "little things."

This started my mind racing . . . all the little things people
consider unimportant which really make a difference. The possi-
bilities are limitless. From grammar to politics.

One thing which all my students know is a pet peeve of mine
is to see "you're" spelled "your." And I would estimate that 90% of
the time, I see it spelled that way on lyric sheets that are given to
me. At the fabulous Austin Expo, where the songs were quite

good, I was amazed to see that 100% of the time, the mistake occurred. "Too" was also written "to" in every single instance.

Of course, a great lyric, misspelled, is still a great lyric. And a bad one is not saved by perfect spelling. It's just that writing is a form of communication, and when one word is substituted for another through ignorance, the communication is altered slightly. Also, the subliminal message is one of "sloppy" or "unprofessional," sort of like the singer singing out of tune or the piano playing out of rhythm. By the way, spell-check on a computer doesn't catch the above two mistakes, because the computer doesn't question the homonym. It merely catches typos.

Anyway, these little things, along with the general presentation of a song—including the production quality of the demo—all add up to a general impression. And some of the ears of today wouldn't be able to ferret out a great song if their lives depended on it. They're used to getting songs in finished master condition. This certainly simplifies their jobs as producers. In some cases, the vocal is merely placed over the master demo track and the only substantial change that's made is in the production credit on the CD liner notes.

Recently I've begun working with someone who has remarkable ears and unusual foresight. He achieved legendary status as a record producer by discovering, developing, choosing songs for and recording hits with Linda Ronstadt, The Beach Boys, Bobby Darin, Sam Cook, Fred Neil, Jim Croce, John Stewart . . . the list is endless. His name is Nik Venet. He not only discovers artists, but songs, as well. He received a copy of Dino Valenti's "Let's Get Together" sung by the writer in such a rough form that, in the background, you could hear the neighbor beating on the wall and telling the writer to stop making so much noise. And yet, in this raw, primitive form, Venet heard the merit of the song. In the 298 albums he's produced, he's discovered a lot of songs, and frequently he was the only voice praising a particular one, until it hit the charts, of course. Nik considers himself a music conservationist in the nineties, protecting "the song" as an endangered species.

I mention this to balance what I said in the beginning about presentation. There are still people around, albeit fewer of them, who can hear a totally unproduced song and appreciate it. And if you find one of them, you've found a person who understands songs and maybe even the art of songwriting itself. A lot of nothingness can be dressed up into somethingness by production. But someone who can hear what's really there by listening to it naked—that's a gift. And one that's rarely found today.

But I'll tell you a couple of places you can find songs being presented this way. One is at the Los Angeles Women In Music Soirees that I host every three months, where songwriter members each sing one or two songs, acoustically, with a guitar or piano. You can really hear the songs this way. These events are very revealing—and extremely entertaining. Also, NAS has begun a series of Gold member concerts at Genghis Cohen on Fairfax in L.A. and for an entire evening you can hear three songwriters present their songs acoustically.

This brings me to the last of the "little things" which are not actually considered very important—and that's melody and lyrics. Oh, I know this sounds controversial, but I can quote you instances—many of them—where the track to a song was worked on for days and days. Then the track was given to the singer whose job it was to "come up with some words" and, when the company was questioned about who was writing the melody, they derisively explained that the singer would think of something.

Well, I have sat riveted as I listened to some of the best songwriting I've heard in ages, coming from the stage at Genghis Cohen on NAS Gold night. When Brock Walsh performed, I was so obviously devastated by the exceptional quality of lyrics he had written, that Steve Schalchlin announced to the whole room, after Brock's show, that Harriet Schock was so overwhelmed, she was getting out of the business. At first I was embarrassed that I had been so noticeably affected and had no doubt made a spectacle of myself.

But the more I thought about the phrase "getting out of the business," the more deeply I interpreted it. I had been recently re-awakened by my producer, Nik Venet, to the responsibility that talent carries with it—to communicate honestly and courageously from who you really are, despite trends, political winds or other changing fancies. This was already a thorn in my side, slowly poisoning my desire to be in "the business."

Hearing Brock Walsh singing "Nobody's Fool" and "Evolution is a State of Mind" was the last straw. Steve Schalchlin was right. I decided that night to get out of "the business." And back into the art.

20

Listen & Learn

In any art form, the new artist learns by studying the masters. And it's obvious which of these new artists have actually studied the masters and which ones have simply put their hand on a rock and said "I am an artist." (A paraphrase of Mel Brooks in "The 2000 Year-Old-Man" album) But studying other writers can be like going on a snipe hunt if you don't know what you're looking for.

Most writers when they're interviewed cite more than one influence. They may have listened to classical music to study harmonic progression, read 300 years of poetry for the craft of emotional shorthand, and listened to everything from opera to bizarre sounds of traffic to capture that elusive gift called melody. Studying other songwriters will be studying a hybrid, of course, because that songwriter is passing along his influences to you in much the same way that a blue eyed parent passes along a dominant gene of brown eyes. You may be listening to the Beatles for harmony and not know you're getting the Beach Boys, and before them, the Lettermen. Studying Eric Clapton is like getting an intravenous injection of all blues that preceded him. He is a master at digesting the past and then re-creating something eclectic, yet uniquely him.

What I think is interesting though, and something you might want to avoid, is studying someone and getting the wrong lesson from that study. The analogy springs to mind of a story attributed to Marilyn Monroe and Einstein. The former allegedly suggested to the latter that they have children who would have her body and his brains. Einstein reportedly refused on the grounds that they might have his body and her brains. (This story is no doubt apocryphal, because Marilyn Monroe was actually very bright. I can't speak for Einstein's body.) Anyway, to study Harry Chapin for his storytelling would be helpful. To study Lionel Richie for his easy melodic sense and to study Tori Amos for the use of lyric visuals would be useful. But to study Harry Chapin for melody, Lionel Richie for lyrical depth or Tori Amos for linear logic would be useless if not downright catastrophic. And that's not to the discredit of these writers. Their known strengths simply lie in the other areas.

I continually see songwriters drawing warped conclusions from studying other songwriters. Just because you may not be able to understand the story line in a Bob Dylan, Sting or Tori Amos song does not mean first of all that no one can. And it certainly doesn't mean you should set about writing songs that no one understands. But time after time, I hear writers defend gobbledygook by saying "Well, Sting does it." No, Sting doesn't do it. You may not know the allusions he's using or have read enough to grasp the context, so you may not understand everything he writes. But remember he also wrote "Every Breath You Take." Can you write that? And are you now purposefully choosing a different style as he is? Or are you clinging to an example of something you don't understand in order to defend your own inability to communicate clearly? He is writing in a chosen style, not out of his limitations. And the way Picasso got there, and James Joyce, and all the other greats who have moved into a less representational style, is through representationalism. Picasso could paint your picture to look like a photograph. Can you write a song that everyone understands and which knocks people out consistently? Only then should you allow yourself to move into deeper waters.

The confusion between being profound and simply being obscure is rampant among beginning songwriters. After all, songwriting is a language we learn. If we've spoken it long enough, we become fluent. Then you can speak of deeper subjects in an impressionistic way. But if your vocabulary in this new language consists of "See Jane run," and "The book is on the table," it may not be a good idea to discuss the meaning of life yet. And this goes for melody as well as lyric. If you don't speak the language of melody and harmony fluently, why would you want to burden yourself with melodic, harmonic or rhythmic goals way beyond your ability to hear or feel? For instance, a writer who can't pick out a classic folk or country melody, will sometimes still try to write something extremely challenging simply because he always liked Steely Dan. If you want to build a muscle, you do a few more lifts each session, then you add more weights. You don't start by giving yourself a hernia.

So listening is extremely important. But equally important is listening in the right place for the right thing. And, as my friend, Gerry Hallford, in Texas used to say, "You can't get all your raccoons up the same tree." You might want to study a lot of different sources, much the way you took different classes in school. Your Math professor didn't teach you English, but you learned from each of them. Luckily, we have a vast and varied sea of music behind us, all of which can teach us something. And for those of us who live in a city where we spend a chunk of the day driving, we're lucky enough to be able to spend that time learning, also. Just think, if you were learning to be a better accountant, all that drive time would be wasted.

21

Character Studies

EOPLE-WATCHING IS A POPULAR PASTIME. Have you ever wondered why? I have. Why would people go to an airport or a park and consider it recreational to watch other members of their species? Maybe it's because people are relentlessly fascinating. And if they're interesting from a distance, how much more obsessed might we become if we knew them intimately? Character studies in songs deal with both the close-up and the far shot.

When you write a song about someone else, have you ever found that it's easier to write about someone you don't know extremely well? There's so much to say about someone you know intimately, you can't possibly get all into a 3-minute song. Of course, you could choose one facet to explore about the person. Or you could write about the character in metaphor. I wrote a song which I recorded on my "American Romance" album, called "Coyote." I was trying to write about someone who was way too big for a song, so I wrote about an animal which carries with it an entire set of similar characteristics. It's a little like dragging an icon on a computer, and carrying a whole set of information with it that gets dropped when you drop the icon down. It's building vertically where you can't spread out. And in a 3-minute song, you don't have the luxury 90 minutes as you do in a film. So you have

77

to pack meaning in a small space. Sometimes that means writing on more than one level.

In the song, "Coyote," I'm talking about the animal, yes. But I'm also talking about a group of people the animal represents, as well as about one particular person—the person who inspired the song by discussing the coyote with me. When he talked about the coyote, all the qualities he mentioned were qualities he, himself, had. I interpreted them in this lyric:

> "The coyote sees us come and go
> He watches from the dark
> We can only imagine what he must know
> And how it breaks his heart
> He's outlasted all of his family
> And the dreamers who shared his dream
> And for better or worse, he sees what is
> Right through the way it may seem..."

I was writing about a visionary, who always takes a back seat, never takes the credit, whose hard-won wisdom has helped him survive, but has left him lonely and sad. It continues,

> "The Coyote howls
> When the sun goes down
> That one more day is lost
> And yet he survives
> To teach us all
> But at what a cost
> To the coyote."

Another way of packing layers of meaning into a character study is by letting the character depict you, yourself, in some way. I recently saw the movie, "Nell" and I was very moved by it. I also had a realization watching it. I was in New Mexico preparing to hand out music and songwriting awards at the 7th Annual Mic

Awards celebration, so my mind was on songwriting. I discovered a principle of good writing by watching the film, and seeing us see Nell (Jodi Foster) through the eyes of the other two main characters. If it had just been a movie about Nell, it would have still been interesting. But what deepened its meaning was that we saw Nell through the eyes of two characters who were seeing themselves in Nell. Each of them was looking at a part of himself/herself which Nell so clearly tapped. This made us even more interested, because all of the characters are revealing something about human nature, and we are discovering ourselves in the process. So when people hear a character study song you write, their interest will be much keener if when you describe the character, you reveal a part of yourself in the process. Anything else is simply documentary.

Just go through daily life, some time, and do this experiment. People watch, and then notice whom you're watching and ask yourself why. Or go through an art book of portraits. Some faces will catch your attention. Ask yourself what you see in the character. Then see if you're really examining your own personality by this process. Recently, I was at a music business fund raiser, on a beautiful day at an exquisite home in Bellaire, California. Everyone was schmoozing up a storm and genuinely enjoying it. I looked out by the swimming pool and there was one guest, sitting on a chaise lounge, all alone, talking on his cellular phone. I couldn't stop watching him. Why would he pay $100 to come to this gorgeous home, ignore the company of charismatic people, just to sit there alone, on the telephone? He could have done that at home, I thought. It finally occurred to me how much of my day I spend isolated, alone and on the telephone. It wasn't something that I felt was significant enough to write a song about, but it made me wake up to the idea that sometimes we're interested in other people to the degree that we, ourselves, are reflected in them. Of course, our listeners are no less egocentric. So we need to give them a shot of themselves by revealing ourselves in the person we're describing. The ripples in the pool just keep expanding.

Nik Venet talks about character studies as parallel to the opening credits of a film being over a still photograph. There are two ways, he says, to get more information from the still photo: 1) You can pull back to reveal more and more of the scene or 2) You can have the characters in the photo begin to move. In a song, you can keep adding to the picture you start the song with, telling us more and more about the character. Or you can simply give us the opening visual and have the person "do" something which will reveal character.

But the most important thing, Venet says, is for the camera to pan around to the person telling the story before the end of the song. There are two parts to this: 1) You write the narrator into the story, giving his/your own viewpoint toward the character or how you know the character (e.g. Bernie Taupin's bringing himself into the lyric of "Candle in the Wind," saying he would like to have met Norma Jean) and 2) You reveal parts of yourself reflected in the character, that you have in common with the character. (e.g. No doubt, Don Henley and Glenn Frey revealed qualities of their own, as well as qualities in all of us, when they wrote "Desperado.") The second one need not be verbalized. But if you know this information, as a writer, the song will have more truth and depth, because whom do you know better than yourself?

That's when the camera turns into a mirror. That's when everybody really gets interested. And that's when the close-up begins.

22

You Talkin' to Me?

"YOU TALKIN' TO ME?" Robert De Niro says in "Taxi Driver." And that's the way I feel when I hear a song that's supposed to be directed at me, the listener, and yet it's a pill I refuse to swallow. Two things come to mind as the culprit: 1) When a song is preachy, I immediately tune out and 2) When it's so in my face and accusational, I refuse to identify with the person the singer is blasting or describing. The singer may be "talkin' to me," but I'm not listening.

So how do we get the listener to swallow the pill, to identify with the person who's being straightened out, to become enlightened? After all, some songs actually make us better people, and how does the writer do that? Well, I can think of four songs right off the bat that have done that for me. John Prine's "Hello In There," so affected me when I first heard it, that it actually changed my behavior. I recently heard it again at a Bette Midler concert and I was moved by it again, as I am every time I hear it. When I walk down the street and pass an elderly person, I take Prine's suggestion and say "Hello" in there. I was not totally oblivious to the situation before I heard the song, but it awakened me more so and somehow gave me permission or a mission. If he had simply screamed at us for ignoring old people, we would have

81

tuned it out. But when you hear the song, you'll hear how sweetly he seduces us to his viewpoint and how safe he makes it for us to agree with him. Great writing does that.

Joni Mitchell in "Trouble Child" paints a picture of a person who's as crazy at that moment as I sometimes feel. So, when I hear it, I don't feel like I'm the only one who's "under the thumb of the maid," or who needs love so badly yet can't give it, or whatever set of aberrations is biting me at the moment. So specific and reveal-ing is the lyric, and yet so brilliantly pointed inward, that we race to identify with it. "That's me," we say. "I break like the waves at Malibu. I feel just like that." The specificity of the confession (even though it's told in the second person) is what helps us find ourselves in it. She doesn't dwell in this song on the disasters we wreak on others when we're in this shape, but we feel secure in going down that trail of thought in the privacy of our cars, or wherever the radio brings us the song.

Bob Dylan can nail a person in a song just about better than anyone. And when he's nailing you, you know it. How many times have those of us of the feminine gender heard "She takes . . . she makes love . . . she aches . . . just like a woman . . . but she breaks just like a little girl" and felt really awful (in a good way, of course)? We see those childish, bratty parts of ourselves that have left a trail of broken pieces, and no matter how together we think we have it, we know that Dylan has seen our worst side. That's why I love Dylan's response to the interviewer who was defend-ing the cover version of the song that changed the lyric to "she breaks up just like a little girl." The interviewer assured him the artist was simply doing her version of it. Dylan's repeated re-sponse was, "No. She got it wrong." And I have to agree. The difference between "breaks" and "breaks up" is pivotal. He meant "breaks."

Perhaps the most successful song I've heard at awakening us to things about ourselves that are difficult to look at is "Secret Garden" by Bruce Springstein. He doesn't rail at a woman for withholding herself, beg for sympathy or position himself as victim. He simply speaks to another man, as if he's giving the sagest advice in the world. He warns him that she'll "let you in her house . . . in her car . . ." but that however you may hunger for the nourishment of true intimacy with her, it will always remain "a million miles away." By the third time I heard this, I wanted to scream "mea culpa!" and throw myself on the ground like Audrey Hepburn in "A Nun's Story," begging his forgiveness, as well as the forgiveness of every man who has ever been left hungry by any woman. The music is such a beautiful, soft carrier wave for the communication and the lyric is so matter-of-fact and non-accusing. He gives us the space to confess, to look at what we do and, who knows? Maybe even to change.

Look at the power of great songwriting. It can wake us up, make us see ourselves as we are at moments when we like to be the most asleep to our true selves. It can change our attitudes and behaviors. It can change the way nations think and perceive the world. And, perhaps most important, it can change the individual and inspire him/her to be more caring. Anyone who thinks songwriting is a frivolous profession is simply doing it wrong.

23

Judging Your Own Material

I HAD A REALIZATION RECENTLY at a songwriters' showcase I was
hosting. The talent for judging one's material comes later than
the talent for writing it.

Having observed for years that becoming a great songwriter
was a most formidable task, I assumed nothing could take longer.
Even if it took additional time to become a wonderful performer,
I thought that would be the last step, that the rest of the package
would just fall together. From then on, I thought, it would be a
matter of growing in what you had to say and saying it well. If you
could do all that, surely you could put a great set together, select
your own material for your CDs, and know which songs to put on
your compilation demo tapes. But this seems to require another
skill, altogether, and just because someone is a great songwriter
and an incredible performer, that doesn't mean he has this other
skill. It is the skill of judging one's own material, of deciding which
song is exceptional and which song is just good. I'll go so far as to
say the skill of telling exceptional from absolutely awful is sometimes missing.

Frequently I've heard publishers, producers and record executives say "He/she's inconsistent." Now I realize more than ever
what that means. It can mean the songs are not at a consistently

84

high level or that within one song, the quality varies. Have you ever heard a song with a great first verse and chorus, and the second verse is from Mars? I often hear a song that barely makes sense until it gets to the killer chorus, which is wasted on a song with lame verses.

A real record producer, and by that I mean, someone who is wearing the hat of a producer—not simply an engineer who's making it all sound good—a real record producer will choose or help choose the songs on a CD. Even at the level of Michael Jackson, when Quincy was producing him, I heard that Quincy sent Michael back time and time again for more songs. When Jackson was interviewed regarding the success of "Thriller," he commented, "We just found the best melodies we could find..." Well, the "we" included Quincy. And lyrics were also seriously considered. So it's not just neophytes who have problems distinguishing between their songs, in quality.

Nik Venet always chooses the material for his artists, and in many cases, gets the artists to write the needed songs in the first place. Since he's not the writer, Venet feels he has a perspective the writer can't possibly have. John Stewart, Fred Neil and Dory Previn always looked to him to choose the material for this very reason. In the case of "California Bloodlines," John Stewart had 30 or 40 songs to choose from. Venet was looking for just the right short stories to make up the novel. Even though John's song, "Daydream Believer" was a hit, it wasn't right for that album, so Venet didn't include it. The vision to see the entire forest is often difficult for the artist who's so close to all the trees. Frequently a more external perspective is necessary. That could account for why so many of the self-produced CDs out there have no continuity; and there is a wide inconsistency in quality between cuts.

Some writer/artists depend upon their live audiences to give them feedback. And this feedback is valuable, to be sure. But what works in concert is sometimes quite different from what will work on a CD. I got talked into recording a show-stopper type of song on my third album, and I really regretted it. It was humorous and the crowds loved it. But it no more matched the rest of the songs on the album than a pink boa would go with a black suit.

Some of the reasons I think writers fall in love with their homely children are: 1) They're new and every new song is the best song you've ever written . . . 2) It feels really good to sing it . . . 3) The circumstances of writing it were exceptional (e.g. It was the only good thing to come out of a bad relationship. . . . It was the first song you wrote with so-n-so. . . . It was the only song you wrote on your vacation in Bermuda. . . . It evokes lots of pictures of your life you like to look at, but which you left out of the song . . . etc.) 4) You've been asked to do a 30 minute set, and you only have 20 minutes worth of good songs.

Although judgment is something gradually acquired and not easily taught, I will suggest a possible way to start. Find your best song—the song that never lets you down, or anyone else down. It could be the song everyone asks for, the one you would show someone who really wanted to know you as a songwriter, but had only 3 or 4 minutes. It's not necessarily the most "hit" sounding song; but it the song that captures most people when they hear it. Ask yourself what's in that song. What is it about the melody, the chords, the rhythm, the story, the pictures, the subject matter— really look at that song in depth. Get into the experience someone has when they hear that song. Does that magic occur with your other songs? If so, to what degree? Use your magical song as a measuring stick. Maybe all the others don't come up to that highest mark, but is there substantial merit, in how it affects listeners and you?

I have a student from Illinois who sends me songs to critique, and part of what he wants is for me to tell him which ones he should show, which ones he should re-write and show, and which ones he should consider learning experiences and discard. In his most recent note, he said "If you ever water down your opinion on my songs, you'll never hear from me again." Since I had been exceptionally frank with him, I was glad he still felt that way. He apparently is aware that he is not the best judge and wants someone else's opinion. Such is not the case with many of the songwriters I see performing or whose tapes I receive. On the same tape will be a masterpiece and a cause for embarrassment. And now I realize it's simply because the skill of distinguishing between the two is learned later, in most cases, than the skill of creating the masterpiece.

24

Everyday Treasures

I USED TO THINK OF MYSELF as some kind of lightning rod, waiting to catch the inspiration and direct it where I needed it. Only important subjects, please. And I truly believed if I just sat in one place long enough, and shut out the rest of the world, it would find me. Wham! I would catch the lightning and I would find a way to translate this earth shattering insight into four minutes of music and lyric.

The worst of it was that I was so busy searching for lightning, I missed a lot of songs along the way. I've met and worked with a number of amazing writers who have demonstrated clearly the importance of the everyday. Nik Venet stresses in his workshop, and with The Campfire Conspiracy, the importance of keeping a journal. He also suggests a reading list with storytellers like Raymond Carver, who tells stories of the everyday where the main characters don't change into celebrities at the end of each story or grow up to become royalty or millionaires. They pretty much stay the same as when they started. But the stories are told in such lifelike detail, the reader changes.

Robert Thornburg, one of the Campfire's favorites, has written a song called "Superbowl Sunday," which says,

"The sun's been up for hours
I have no eggs or bread
I could drive to the market
But I decide to walk instead.
And as I walk I see things
Things I've never seen before
Like the pretty little girl in the dumpster
And her brother outside the store."

Audiences are spellbound as this story unfolds, showing the little girl in the dumpster letting loose a spiraling head of lettuce which little brother, going deep and cutting back, catches and laterals to grandma who spikes it into the shopping cart.

This song is so well known among the Sunday Night Campfire audiences that Bruce Larsen jokes with them that he himself ran to the store, hurried by some little girl in a dumpster and her family, and got back home as soon as he could so he could work on a song he'd been thinking about. And that's what most people do, seriously. They miss the songs in life, because they're so busy thinking about writing.

Sarah Kim Wilde writes,

"Sittin' at the Kmart Counter
Wishin' I had more mustard,
And more money and more time. . . .
A broken man walks over;
I play I haven't noticed,
But I can't ignore
The soft tapping on my arm and
He says, 'Little miss,
Is this seat taken?
And have you found the Good Lord Jesus?
You're lookin' so alone...'"

The story she tells is short, full of pictures . . . an everyday story, and yet in less than three minutes, she reveals more about herself and life than most people do in a novel.

Steve Wagner writes about high school days with a friend named Danny:

"He'd get me at eight
And we'd head to this place,
Out where the road turned to dirt.
He'd have a beer,
And he'd disappear
Hot on the trail of a skirt.
He wasn't that brave;
The one thing that saved him
Was knowing a more frightened man.
So I'd hold his place
And tell him, 'Go get her, ace,'
Then I would clap for the band."

First of all, the everyday is full of pictures because they're there, part of the physical world that surrounds us. When we start waxing poetic and philosophical, even emotional, we sometimes lose the pictures. Great writers frequently use the everyday pictures to deliver the emotion. That way the listener discovers and unravels the emotion or the philosophy by looking at the pictures, rather than having it telegraphed, as he might by a lesser writer.

Bill Berry, Jim Dean and Martha Moore have a song called, "Pecan Pie," about an attempt at rekindling an old flame which says:

"She walks into the bedroom,
I stand at the door;
Nothing's movin' but the ceiling fan.
I lie down beside her
In a comfortable spoon,
She traces circles on the back of my hand."

Of course, 100 people can see a movie and come away with 100 different interpretations; imagine how many different stories 100 different writers could come away from real life with, even observing the same scene. It's a veritable "Rashamon." That's where unique viewpoint and style come in.

The Farmers' Market on 3rd and Fairfax in Los Angeles is a wonderful place to observe the everyday. People from all over the world come there as tourists. Elderly comedians have lunch and try to top each other with one-liners. Unnatural-orange-haired ladies stand in line for an entire lunch break just to buy one lottery ticket or scratch-off, only to complain publicly and loudly when it doesn't bring them the fortune they expected. The shoe shine man has seen it all and isn't telling. And everywhere there's an impending feeling of tenuousness - like it could all be torn down at a moment's notice to make way for a high rise. In a city which witnessed Ship's Restaurants closing in 1995, one gets the feeling that nothing is sacred. And for a songwriter to lose a place like the Farmer's Market, it would be like a farmer losing his top soil.

Even if we do no more than train our powers of observation, we can start finding the magic in the everyday, whether we write about it or simply learn to witness it. We may choose to write about the deepest of issues and emotions, but the pictures will come from the regular old world around us. From the everyday. And every day we don't observe them, we could be missing an opportunity to discover a treasure.

25

Finding the Pony

*I*N CASE YOU HAVEN'T HEARD THE STORY about the son who asked his parents for a pony every year, I will tell the shortened version. So harassed by the child every Christmas for a pony, the parents decided this Christmas to play a cruel trick on the son. They purchased a large burlap bag of horse manure and put it under the tree. On Christmas morning, they came downstairs to find him shoveling it into the living room fast and furiously. "What are you doing?" they screamed in horror. "With all this horse manure, there's bound to be a pony in here somewhere," the boy replied.

I have thought of this story more times than I can count, as I've sat with students, collaborators and colleagues looking for the songs in the long, often fascinating stories of their lives. It's a little like the children's puzzle where the page is filled with dots or any repeating pattern, and you're supposed to find the bird or the cat or dog in the pattern. Once you find it, it's hard to believe you couldn't see it before. But it sometimes takes a trained eye to find it. Sometimes we're just too close to our own stories to see the poetry in them, or the point, or the lesson. Frequently non-writers have things happen to them which are sheer poetry. It's just that they seldom know it. The realization, the metaphor, the song is just sitting there, biting them on the nose. But they don't recognize it. Then a songwriter comes along, hears it and is knocked out by the power of the story. And a song is born.

Generally if you're getting the story from someone else's life, it's helpful to totally immerse yourself in what actually happened. And, if possible, relate it to something in your own life. The truth that makes the big difference between art and fluff will be there in both your lives, and without it, it's just another song written around "a good idea," as Nik Venet talks about in his workshop.

So how do you find the kitten in the dots, and realize the pony may be nowhere near the bag of manure? Or how do you find the pony *in* the bag of manure? Well, it's helpful to have another person to bounce it off of, and if that person knows which questions to ask, you're on your way. A new student of mine, Matt Hennager, came to me with a story about how a girl broke his heart because he was really in love with her, and she kept crying on his shoulder about other guys. Of course, this story has been written before, but not his story, in particular. So I got him to talk to me about it and we talked and talked and talked. Eventually, he said some things that determined the direction of the song. Two prospective titles came out: "The hero didn't win this time," and "Why not love me, instead." These two songs would be developed quite differently. So finding the song within the story required some specific questions. For the first title, I asked him what he did that was like a hero—give me examples of times she really tested his patience and understanding, times he came through for her with valiant actions, times he was obviously "the good guy." He would get off on other tangents about the relationship, because that's natural. But I would just keep bringing him back to the topic at hand. For the second title, "Why Not Love Me Instead," I asked him to tell me times she treated him like a friend, times she said she couldn't have made it without him and other such comments, incidents where she showed her gratitude in ways that made it even harder for him to be her friend and not her lover. Once again, he would start talking about other subjects regarding her, all of which were factual, but would have been red herrings in this particular song. So after a long interview, I sent him off to think about it some more, but to think about it along the lines of the questioning I had put him through. Now he was focused. Now he was writing the song, not just facts about his ex-girlfriend.

Another student named Stephen Mac wanted to write about an experience he had written in his journal. He went to a barber shop where men of an older generation talked among themselves as they listened to Frank Sinatra and Bobby Darin on the radio. That, in itself, didn't seem like a song. In talking about it, he mentioned an uncle of his. I asked him if the men in the barber shop reminded him of his elders, his uncle in particular. He went on to say yes, that his elders had had a tremendous influence on him, and that his uncle had spent a year teaching him to be an electrician's apprentice. During that year, he said, he learned one thing. He learned he had to be a musician—not an electrician. Somewhere in the conversation he said that his uncle "understood a lot about life and mechanical things, and maybe life as a mechanical thing." I stopped him and told him to make a note of that. So what did all this have to do with the men in the barber shop? I asked him to tell me the difference between his experience with the men and his memories of his family. He came to the conclusion which became the concept of the song—the realization, the win, the ending plot point. When he was in the barber shop, he could simply observe and leave it all behind. He walked in free and walked out free, without the baggage he once carried from his elders. In the writing of the song, he may discover the point of freedom came earlier—when he finished his apprenticeship. He hasn't written it yet. So I don't know. I just know that he now has a concept, not just a journal entry. He has a realization and a moment that meant something to him which may be translated into a more universal feeling—freedom from the control of the past. How he uses Frank Sinatra and Bobby Darin's being on the radio, the conversations of the old men, the uncle, the apprenticeship, the comparison of present to past, the feeling of freedom at the end of the incident—these will tell the tale, literally. He will use as many visuals as possible, and if done skillfully, the listener will have the realization along with him. No spoon feeding allowed. Shortly after our discussion, he called with his title, "The Old Standards." I think the concept is in good hands.

Finding the song in the story is actually what a lot of professional songwriters do when they write with an artist who may not be an experienced writer. The artist tells the experience. The songwriter finds the song. Then, when the singer sings it, it's his/her story. Without a professional collaborator, if left up to their own storytelling chops, some artists might tell a true, factual story of their lives. But the audience is left, forever, looking for the pony.

26

He Says, She Says

I DISLIKE GENDER STEREOTYPES, in life and in songs. So I've protested their existence and their use. Recently, though, I've been observing them in song lyrics, especially when it comes to viewpoints during the break-up of a relationship.

Whether a man or a woman has written the song, if the singer is a man, the viewpoint will often be, "What happened? I thought everything was fine." If the singer is a woman, it will often be, " I tried to tell you a hundred times," or "I knew it was falling apart for years." Somehow, trying to reverse these and have the woman sing a song that goes, "You left me a note on the milk carton and that was the first I knew there was a problem" as is the theme of "That Ain't No Way To Go, " seems totally out of character. Similarly, to have a woman espouse the viewpoint suggested in "Phones Are Ringing All Over Town" would not be likely. The character in this song, also a man, is calling "The hospital, friends of hers and his, He knows she'd never leave him, She's just got to be around . . ." but phones are ringing all over town and she's on a plane. Martina McBride is just as convincing singing this as she was singing about the woman who burned the house down on "Independence Day." Somehow we don't see as many clueless wives calling the hospitals when their husbands are on planes leaving them or men burning down the house with the wife in it who abused him.

Now, I know this is going to agitate my colleagues who rage against the notion there is any difference between the sexes. Maybe there really isn't that much difference, but there's difference in the general perception of their viewpoints. People perceive that there is a difference between the usual behavior of a man and a woman when they leave relationships. And for a stereotype to take hold, there is usually some grain of truth in it. Maybe it's caused by environment and circumstances, even prejudice, but it's still the way people are perceived during that time period. The notable exception, of course, to the clueless-man/tried-to-tell-you woman is that Jim Webb's "By The Time I Get To Phoenix" is about a woman who never dreamed he would go. So there are songs that go against the stereotype successfully. When Nik Venet produced "Different Drum," he had Linda Ronstadt sing "I ain't sayin' you ain't pretty, I'm just sayin' I'm not ready for any person, place or thing to try and pull the reins in on me." It was written by a man, Michael Nesmith, but that was one of the first times a woman had made that statement on a record and it made history. Now it's an everyday occurrence.

In "You Can Feel Bad" by Matraca Berg and Timothy Krekel, the woman is telling the man who left her that she saw it coming for a long time, but he can picture her walking around in his old sweater reading his love letters if he needs to. In fact, though, she's doing pretty well. On the other hand, Willie Nelson discusses a break-up by taking some degree of responsibility. He says maybe he didn't do this, maybe he didn't do that . . . the list is quite long . . . but at least he was thinking of her. Somehow I can't hear a woman saying that. If a woman knew there were things she wasn't doing, she would probably not excuse them by saying, "But you were always on my mind." Actually, neither would a lot of men, but the "cowboy" would say that. The romanticized notion of the desperado who never lets anyone too close. That person might reveal enough of himself to admit that even though no action was taken, he really did love her and all the while he wasn't there for her, he was thinking about her. For anyone who's ever loved a cowboy, this turns out to be better than nothing. So the song always makes me cry, in spite of (or because of) the naivete of the viewpoint.

When Bonnie Raitt sings "I Can't Make You Love Me, " she is simply looking at a hopeless situation and coming to terms with it. She'll feel the power when they make love, but he won't. She's not asking for one more night, in order to sway him. She's just seeing it for the way it is. Nik Venet, my mentor and producer, has said that men will want to hear that song because it says what they feel about someone they love. But they will want to hear it sung by a woman.

When Richard Thompson says, "I misunderstood, I thought she was saying 'good luck,' she was saying 'good-bye,'" he uses the cluelessness of his character (himself, in the song) to give irony to the lyric. He does that even more intensely in "Read About Love," where he says "So why don't you moan and sigh? Why do you sit there and cry? I do everything I'm supposed to do, If something's wrong, then it must be you/ I know the ways of a woman, I've read about love." He's a master at achieving irony by taking on the character of someone who doesn't have a clue. I call it the Archie Bunker school of satire. Yes, there are people who thought Archie Bunker was espousing their viewpoints and considered him a hero. They didn't know they were being ridiculed along with him in the TV show "All In The Family." Richard Thompson ridicules a short-sighted point of view by taking it on as his own. But could/would a woman sing that lyric? I don't think so.

An interesting song by Bruce Larsen, called "Flowers Every Sunday," puts a new spin on this stereotype of the clueless guy and has the man saving a relationship by informing himself in time. It would be a disservice to synopsize the lyric, so I'll just quote it all:

"Something happened yesterday when
    just by accident I learned
And I guess that you could say
    I caught my bridge before it burned.
You see, when I picked up the phone,
    she was talking with her friend
And I meant to put it down,
    but something made me listen in.
And I felt childish at the time,
    cause I'm not usually that way
But I noticed she was crying,
    and that's when I heard her say

She said it's almost over, he don't love me anymore
No more walks along the river, or kisses at the door
No more flowers every Sunday, or dancing in the rain
I'd better just go quietly, and save everyone the pain.

With the hours slowly drifting,
    I kept hearing every word
Though I went through all the motions,
    just as if I hadn't heard
I'd thought that she was happy,
    just how blind can one man be
How easily forgotten,
    what the little things can mean.
And as I stared into the darkness
    of a night that wouldn't end
I made myself a promise,
    I'd never hear those words again
'Cause I won't let it be over,
    when every day I love her more
We'll walk along the river,
    and I'll kiss her at the door

She'll have flowers every Sunday,
   dancing every time it rains
And I'll win her heart back quietly,
   and save everyone the pain.
Yes, I'll win her heart back quietly,
   and save everyone the pain."

Of course, there are other break-up songs that rise above gender and give us universal wisdom. Joni Mitchell's "Big Yellow Taxi," parallels what we've done to the world to what we do to each other . . . "Don't it always seem to go . . . that you don't know what you've got till it's gone. . . . They paved paradise and put up a parking lot." And then there's Dylan, who has looked at this subject from all sides. One of my personal favorites is the succinct verse from "Never Gonna Be the Same Again," "You give me something to think about, baby, every time I see ya. Don't worry baby, I don't mind leaving, I'd just like it to be my idea." Henley, Souther, and Campbell take us through every possible emotion in "Heart of the Matter" and leave us with the pearl. "But I think it's about forgiveness, forgiveness, even if, even if you don't love me anymore."

27

Listeners Vote
for Communication

*A*FTER THE PRESIDENTIAL ELECTION, I heard a well-known political analyst make the pronouncement that what wins elections is not platforms and voting records. It's not character or integrity. It's the ability of the candidate to communicate well. The political analyst did not mean precise communication of policy or viewpoint of the candidate, but merely the ability to say something clearly, interestingly and compellingly.

As most things do, this made me think about songwriting. If you compose music that is compelling, interesting and not over everyone's head, people will respond to it emotionally. If what you say is clear enough for them to get something—whether it's precisely what you meant or not—and if you say it in an interesting way and involve them emotionally, you will get their vote. The person could be a listener at a club, a producer looking for outside material, an artist, or merely a record buying fan. All these categories of listeners seem to respond similarly. They don't want to be confounded with illogic or arbitrary chord changes. They don't want to feel like they're sitting at a blank screen, the other side of which is your movie with you watching it; in other words, they don't want to be left out of the experience you're having simply by your inability to communicate it to them. Also, they don't want to be numbed by a string of cliches they've heard a thousand times: the "chicken in every pot" of songwriting.

When you listen to someone give a speech, what do you come away with? Generally I remember the pictures and actual stories they tell. If in telling them, the speaker illustrates a point he/she is making, then I may come away with the point of the speech. Too much songwriting is rhetoric, with no illustration. After it's over, no one knows what all that singing was about. Many times in a workshop, I'll hear a song and at the end of it, I'll wonder to myself, "What was that masked message?" Then I'll ask the other students what the song was about and they'll have no idea. But along comes a song full of pictures, illustrations, stories, analogies and examples, and everyone will know what it was about. Maybe everyone won't know every level on first listening, but people will be able to tell you what the main point was. And they will respond favorably more often than not.

Of course, musical genre and personal taste come into it, as well. A wonderful song in a musical bag antipathetic to the listener is not going to make it. I've occasionally been at showcases where the most brilliant lyric is presented and I'll be elbowing someone next to me to listen to it. She or he will say something like, "I can't get past the music." For those who think lyric is everything, it comes as a great disappointment that there are many audience members who are listening for melody as a prerequisite to the message and/or craft in the lyric. But when the melody is accepted, it becomes the carrier wave that takes a great lyric into the heart of a listener. Then you really have it all.

I think people do want information about the subject of your song, just like they want information regarding the topic of a politician's speech. They may not get it and still come away feeling it was a good speech. But when they start thinking about it, they didn't learn anything new. If the smoke is articulated well, they will like the speaker (songwriter) better than if it's gibberish, but what really pleases the listener is well-articulated substance. I recently had an audience member say he was listening to every word of a song of mine called "For What It's Worth" because he wanted to know how his ex-girlfriend felt. He kept waiting to find a line that wouldn't make him feel like it was her viewpoint, but he didn't find one. Perhaps the reason I succeeded in giving him substance is that it was written honestly from one person's viewpoint (mine) without rhetoric and with down-to-earth pictures and examples. I remember the night well. I didn't win the vote I was going for. But, at least, I helped one person know how his girlfriend felt.

28

That's Entertainment

I'VE COME TO A REALIZATION OVER THE YEARS of listening and observing artists of all kinds: Art can be entertaining; but entertainment is seldom art.

I'm accustomed to making waves when I talk about things, because I'm very straightforward and from Texas. So when I've shared this controversial statement with a few singer/songwriters I know, it has met with mixed response. Some sighed, relieved it all made perfect sense now. And some started shouting at me. The latter group usually consisted of singers who took up writing because they heard it was easier to get a deal if you wrote your own songs. At the heart of them, they're entertainers. And there's nothing wrong with that. But for some reason they don't like to give up the illusion that they're serious artists as well.

That's not to say that singers who rarely write are non-serious artists. There are many singers, like Linda Ronstadt, Sam Cooke, Natalie Cole, Tricia Yearwood, who select(ed) songs reflecting a definite point of view as an artist. That's considerably different from a singer whose prime motive is to create an effect of entertainment on an audience. The entertainer is distracting the audience/listener from life. The artist is creating and communicating about life. There will be a target audience who "gets" what this artist is doing. And the artist may write/sing to them, for them and with them in mind. But the artist is most concerned with the quality of what he is communicating—and that it does communicate, powerfully, provocatively and clearly.

It's is the intention which differs. And this intention results in either art or entertainment. Of course, intention is not sufficient to create an artist. Technical expertise is a must. The writer has to be able to write, the singer to sing, in order for communication to occur. But I would venture to say the writing expertise is more important than the singing, if we're looking for art rather than entertainment. Because a good singer singing a bad song may be entertainment, but it sure ain't art. However, a less than accomplished singer singing a great song has been known to be art. We simply change our criteria for what a singer should sound like when s/he's singing something remarkable. I've heard Nik Venet tell the story of the time he played Bob Dylan's first, yet unreleased album, still on acetate, for Harlan Howard, Hank Cochran, Mary Jon Wilkins and Johnny Cash in the basement of Harlan Howard's house in Nashville in the 60s. They sat in silence, stunned. When it was over, Harlan silently started it from the beginning and they listened to it all the way through again.

I should reiterate here that art can be entertaining. And no one walks that line better than the satirical songwriters like Randy Newman, Marie Cain and Lyle Lovett. People are truly entertained when they hear these artists, but they're also moved, incited, chagrined, appalled, made to examine their values—all sorts of things that entertainment doesn't make a career out of doing. Art does that.

So as an artist, you're look for your target audience. That's who's going to be on your wave length, to get what you're trying to communicate. If you're writing metaphorically with literary illusions, you would probably not find your target audience at dance clubs. And now that people are bypassing the industry, with their clear-cut categories and airplay formats, singer/songwriters are falling into the trap of thinking they can do anything.

The very opposite is true. You really have to know whom you're talking to now, because whether you're selling a CD out of the trunk of your car after live shows or putting sound bytes on the Internet, you have to be better than lots of the other people out there who are bypassing the industry to get to your audience. You have to take your best shot like a laser, not a shotgun. And it better hit the heart of the buyer, or you don't have a chance. Art will do that. Entertainment is over when the lights go down. The effect will not carry over to the ordering of the CD phase, or even to point of purchase or word-of-mouth.

Nik Venet said it so well at a seminar, I will quote him:

"When messages are passed on to an audience and the audience responds, you have created an emotional impact. We are not talking about entertainment . . . watching from a distance, a show for your numbing pleasure. The aware audiences of the nineties, say, 'Don't give us one-way entertainment. You say and do, we watch and do nothing. Don't control us; television controls us. Don't hypnotize or seduce us from our human feelings and responsibilities. We want a two-way process. We need fulfilling experiences for comparisons. Do it and say it without smoke bombs and mirrors. Tell us the simple, unadorned truth and let us, as individual and independent souls, listen to and visualize your songs.'"

As far as I'm concerned, that last statement is art. And he wasn't even holding a guitar when he said it.

29

Smoke and Mirrors

SMOKE AND MIRRORS CAN BE THE MARK of both a good and a bad songwriter, depending upon the kind of smoke, and the use of mirrors. First let's take a look at bad smoke . . . smoke that clouds the issue, smoke that obscures the subject. Songwriters frequently are looking for good smoke (mystery, drama) and fall into the other kind.

Too often I've heard a songwriter point to writing he likes on a CD or the radio and say, "You see? I want to write like that. I'm not sure what he/she meant, but it really affected me." What affected the songwriter was his own story he filled in from the pictures the songwriter on the CD painted—as well as the emotional effect of the melody and harmony. The images in the song may have meant one thing to the writer and may evoke something different in the listener, but that's the beauty of using images. James Taylor meant something other than airplanes in "Fire and Rain" when he said, "Flying machines in pieces on the ground," but we got what we got. So that type of smoke creates a kind of mystery. Great songs are frequently written on more than one level. The literal level tells one story and the metaphoric level tells a story you may not even get until the third of fourth hearing. Some people will never get it. They'll just enjoy that song about the beaches in Wyoming. Twenty years ago, this kind of listener enjoyed hearing what a desperado's life was like when he was out ridin' fences. They buy records, so God bless 'em. But they're probably not anyone's target audience.

Music can create mystery, the good smoke. A melody that goes to an unpredictable place or certain chord changes can create a mood where the listeners hangs on every word. It's best not to disappoint them with lyrics that are obscure, abstract, illogical, or as we'll see, self-centered.

Mirrors are a good thing when they look into the heart of the songwriter, as Nik Venet says in his workshop, "with a tiny flashlight for the hidden corners." He goes on to say:

"The songwriter is really alone . . . a space-saving, territorial person who, on occasions, can be found wandering among us, jotting down journal entries that will become small mirrors that we, the audience, will eventually see ourselves in. For better or for worse, but for real."

The mirror turns on the listener when the songwriter has had the courage and craft to reveal something so personal and specific that it will reveal something about the listener as well. This is an example of the specific becoming universal. This is the kind of mirror Nik Venet is talking about, above. Too often an inexperienced songwriter, in an attempt to have general appeal, will keep his lyric generic. In an attempt to appeal to everyone, he will touch no one.

Everybody is the center of his own universe. A great songwriter will speak about the listener's universe by digging deep into his own heart and mind to find those truths that others are afraid to face or can't find their way to. These shared realizations move the listener, make him feel he's part of the human race. The less interested, and therefore less interesting, songwriter will write about himself because that's all he's really interested in. His lyrics will deal with such introspective subjects as how angry he/

she is that the lover left . . . how he's going to show the world his true worth . . . why he has such bad luck . . . and how confused he is by all the mysteries of life. The mysteries of life could range from why he lost his job to why his parents were so thoughtless.

As the excellent songwriter/singer, Kevin Fisher of Naked to the World, said to me at the Acoustic Underground Anniversary Concert, "There are no bad subjects. . . ." It's true—any of these "self-indulgent" subjects listed above, in the hands of a skillful writer, could dazzle us. But in the hands of a writer whose mirror is always seeing his own adoring face, the subject will seem shallow, poorly written and not relevant to most people. So as the audience begins to talk among themselves, the songwriter gets a subject for his new song . . . "why they didn't listen." Pretty soon, we feel like we're in a house of mirrors with that songwriter's face in every mirror. It's more like a nightmare.

So next time you're listening to smoke and mirrors, ask yourself what kind each is. If there's a haunting, mysterious melody and harmony setting a lyric that draws you in and makes you think and feel, it's good smoke. And if you start looking at your life and the pictures in your head by listening to the writer reveal his own specific dilemmas, dreams, realizations . . . it's a good mirror. That's what art is for. Honor that writer. But if there's obscurity thinly veiling the self-centered attempt at oral angst, don't even stay long enough to buy a drink. Go home and put on a CD that inspires you.

Part III

Technology

30

Words or Music . . .
That Is the Question

*P*EOPLE LIKE TO DEBATE WHICH IS MORE IMPORTANT, music or lyrics. Lyricists love the story about Oscar Hammerstein's wife, Dorothy, overhearing Jerome Kern's wife insisting that Jerome Kern wrote "Ol' Man River" and Dorothy said, "No, your husband wrote bom, bom, bom, bom, (5-5-6-1) . . . MY husband wrote 'Ol' Man River.'" Composers like to note that everyone can hum their melodies, and even they, themselves, need lyric sheets if they're asked to play at a party, because "no one remembers the words."

Having been a lyricist to composers and a composer to lyricists, I can argue both sides. And because I see the importance of both, I like to explain my view of it with the following analogy: Let's say for argument's sake you're a guy at a party. You see a beautiful girl and you start talking to her. In the course of the conversation, she says something insightful or unusual. She sparks your interest in her as a person, not just another pretty face. You want to get to know her better.

To me, this is the way it is with music and words. The music (the girl's physical beauty) is what first got the guy's attention. But if she'd been incredibly stupid or self-centered and talked about herself all the time and was not interested in him at all, he probably would have walked away after a while. A good lyric that makes the listener feel something and/or learn something about himself is likely to get past first base. An illogical, self-indulgent, or banal lyric with a great melody or groove will not have the life that a great melody AND great lyric would have.

I hear students and other friends say "But listen to this lyric" and point to something on the radio that has all the "the"s and "a"s accented in the music and is held together more with political glue than a logical thread. But let's see how often that song would get cut if the producer or artist hadn't written it.

Back to our analogy, the most wonderful, brilliant girl at the party, who has no appealing physical presentation—either because she stands in the dark or she came in her house shoes and hot rollers—this girl has little chance of being discovered. Unfortunately, the same could be said of a brilliant lyric with a mundane melody or tedious track. People hear feel first, melody second and lyric last—or so it seems, in my experience.

So what does all this mean? And who cares, anyway? Well, I think it's important to face this fact, especially if you're a mediocre melody writer with a great gift for lyric. And if that is the case, there are a number of things you can do to improve the situation. First of all, you can isolate the melody, before you fall irrationally in love with it by putting those golden lyrics with the notes. Listen to it, naked, in all its vulnerability. See if it makes the hair on your own neck stand up without the words. Many people who have studied with me have had to face this type of melodic scrutiny at least once a semester. So one does survive it. It's much easier to alter its shape, its rhythm, its harmonic structure in its raw form. Then, after you have a killer melody, it's worth putting words to. Secondly, you could collaborate with a really good composer.

If you write great melodies and think as long as you speak English, you're a lyricist, you may also be in for a rude awakening. Learning, honing, improving and perfecting the art of lyric writing (or the Craft as Sheila Davis so aptly writes) can be a lifelong journey. Knowing what type of lyric to put with what type of track and melody, how to put it to the notes, how to shape the story, how to turn the knife of irony at the perfect time to affect the listener exactly the way you want to—these are things that raise the song to the level of real communication rather than merely throwing notes and words into the atmosphere.

Of course, some people write all the lyrics first. Provided this is done to a rhythm of some sort, it can work well for songwriters. It allows them to get the best possible lyric written without regard to the constraints of a melody. But it helps to know both approaches. One of my former students and now a successful songwriter for film and television, Barbara Jordan, came to my workshop having written lyric first, exclusively. She was horrified to hear she was going to write melody first. (The lyricists who study with me, like Ron Troutman, merely bring in lyrics. I don't force everybody to write melodies, although I've helped a few lyricists become songwriters by doing just that.) Barbara discovered a whole new way of writing by concentrating on the melody before either writing the lyric or giving it to a lyricist. Now she has the choice of writing to a lyric or writing the melody first. She actually prefers writing melodies without words, now, and then brainstorming the lyric with someone else.

The main arguments for writing the lyric after the melody are: 1) You usually get a stronger melody when it's written unencumbered by a lyric; 2) a great melody will force a lyric to be streamlined and condensed; and 3) when the lyricist dictates the rhythm of the melody, he or she is actually doing the composer's work, and frequently the results are not very musical. (I know Elton and Bernie wrote this way, but Bernie Taupin also writes music, so he no doubt heard a rhythm in his head when he was writing the lyric.)

Once the melody and track are powerful on their own, then comes the challenge of putting words to it that will bring home the emotional impact the music is meant to have. In country songs, the lyric carries more than 50% of the weight in most cases. But in all genres, the lyric has the task of fulfilling the promise of the music. And it can be the difference between a 5-minute conversation, as in our previous analogy, or a marriage that lasts a lifetime.

So the debate goes on, like the battle of the sexes. Perhaps they're both out of date. What really matters is that both elements emerge strong and memorable. I think they can help each other get there.

3 1

Writing Words to Music

As I said in "Words or Music, that is the Question," writing lyrics without a melody to write them to is a risky business—because you're setting the rhythm of the melody, rather than letting the melody do that. So, some people have asked me how you actually put words to music that already exists. I have to say that I've been doing it so long—since about the sixth grade—that I'm not sure what's the best way to help another person develop that skill. Even when I write the lyric first, I generally write a verse and chorus before I set it to a melody. So the second verse is always written to a melody, no matter how I start the song, with melody or with lyric. I find it amusing that songwriters who write words and music simultaneously sometimes say they could never write to a melody, and yet they write the second and third verses to a melody routinely.

If I'm given a melody with no lyrics at all and no title, I think it's easiest for me to start with finding the title in the melody. Determine where that is and come up with a title and concept you really love. Then, find where the sections of the song are and find where the music is rhyming. By that I mean, find out which notes are in a repeated sequence, rhythmically, although they may be on different actual notes (Like "yesterday" and "far away" in the first line of the song "Yesterday") This will determine your rhyme scheme, although it won't be etched in stone.

Now, before you start pouring the lyric into the melody, be sure you've spent some time in your viewpoint and either know WHAT you're going to say or where you're coming from as the person who's speaking. Otherwise, you'll always sound like you're "outside" the song and you'll end up writing lyrics that sound like "lyrics" and draw the attention of the listener away like bad acting draws people out of the movie.

Of course, you also have to make sure the words sing well—that's probably the most important thing of all. Make sure the syllables that are accented in the music are what would be accented in speaking. You can't distract the listener with words that don't flow well with the music. This means that if you're writing up-tempo songs with lots of 16th notes, you'd better keep the consonants down to a minimum. Find combinations of words that roll off the tongue really easily and naturally with not a lot of stops. We're not lucky enough to write in a Romance language like Spanish or French. English is a Germanic language and lots of things stop the flow of air. Maybe the reason why lines like "All I really wanna know" appear so often in dance tunes, is that they flow without stops on the air current. On the other side of the coin, "Would he make me stop and ask" in the same melody would give both singer and the listener a nervous tick.

Maybe that's why we hear that "Ham and Eggs" was the original dummy lyric to "Yesterday." Working with nonsense syllables can sometimes just get words that sing well into the spaces and break the silence barrier. From there, you can start writing the real lyric. At this point, all the principles of good writing should be applied. I cannot stress enough knowing what you want to say BEFORE you start filling in the melody notes with syllables.

I see songwriting as similar to parenting. No one's really experienced in or prepared for it when we start. And we all just find our way. By the time we master it, the children are grown and the songs that embarrassed us early in our careers have, hopefully, been replaced by our newer work.

32

"What, Me Study?"

ACTORS ARE SOME OF MY BEST STUDENTS, because they are accustomed to the idea of studying their craft. First of all, they can't do it alone in their living rooms . . . without seeming a bit odd. So they need a class to work out and practice their craft. Songwriters, on the other hand, can sit at home and write a song. They don't need to be hired first, or be in a class or workshop. They can sit there and write a song, then go to an open mike and play it. And many songwriters have been doing this for years, never studying the craft at all. Naturally, many have learned on their own by keen observation of what great writers are doing, by reading great poets and novelists and by listening to inspired compositions of various genres. But, then this is study, too.

Unfortunately, though, many songwriters don't even do that. The art form, (and I insist that it is), is simply too "easy" to do. You get a guitar and a piece of paper, put some words and notes together and sing it for your friends. That's all there is to it for some. As my mentor and producer, Nik Venet says, "If paper cost $100 a sheet and a pencil weighed 25 pounds, there would be a lot fewer songs written. And that wouldn't necessarily be a bad thing."

So when an actor asks to study with me, I'm always glad. At least he/she will understand the value of learning the craft. Of course, there are actors who get hired before they know how to act or struggle through their years on the soaps, but actors don't have near the opportunities to get up and bore people to death that songwriters do. They have worked so hard on their acting by the time they get a chance to act in front of a room full of people, they are prepared. And if they're not, there are hundreds of others who are who will probably get the part instead. But at an open mike, which doesn't require auditions, anybody can get up and sing anything, and often that is what seems to be happening these days.

Milton Katselas's acting classes are filled with very well known actors, as well as not-yet-knowns. Stars continue to work at their craft, pushing the envelope and meeting new challenges in order to keep growing. I think many already good songwriters do this too, but maybe in the beginning stages, more should. At first, it's such a thrill to a writer to finish a song, he wants to run into the studio, which could also be in his living room, and record it. It's appalling to think of the funds and tape devoted to songs that wouldn't fly if they had a running start off a cliff. And yet these same beginning writers who would be embarrassed to admit they need help are not embarrassed at all to stand up in public and sing these songs, or play the tapes.

There is so much excellent talent around, it doubles the crime of not developing it. If the singer/songwriters playing out were without promise, it would just be another tedious experience to hear them. But sometimes a flash of brilliance will catch your attention and the lack of follow through can break your heart. Frequently just the slightest tweaking would bring the entire song home. And to hear the song three months later, without any rewriting occurring, is for someone like me, like fingernails on a blackboard.

What I've noticed at so many of the open mikes is the same people playing over and over and not getting any better because they're not being challenged, not being given direction. They're dragging the same weaknesses around with them they've had since they started writing and they don't even know what they are. Then the new crop of writers pops up and some of them get better and some don't. When one actually works on his craft, he stands out like a jewel among the rest. That alone should make the others take note and wonder what he's doing. But perhaps the same blindness that pervades that oblivious writer's thinking, that keeps him from studying in the first place, keeps him from asking the gem who just sang what he's been doing to get so good. The frightening truth could be that the "independent" writer, who's proud to say he learned everything in his own living room, can't actually tell the difference between what he's doing and what the really good writers are doing. So he doesn't know whose work to admire and learn from. He doesn't know when to go up to somebody and say, "Why are you so good?" So he'll never hear anybody say, "I've been studying."

33

Melody—The Unsung Hero

*N*OW THAT THERE'S A DEMAND for intelligent songs again (see Feb. 28, 1994 Business Section of *The New York Times* regarding the change in radio formats, Adult Album Alternative), everyone talks about lyrics. That's vitally important to me, as well. I'm not called the "lyric police" for nothing. But those who know me well also refer to me as the "melody police." I guess that's because I'm always lobbying for melody, reminding people of the importance of it, trying to help students strengthen melodies and create more emotionally impactful ones. Let's face it, the greatest lyric in the world is never going to be heard over an extremely weak melody. Strangely enough, the reverse of this isn't true. There are plenty of songs on the radio with great melodies and atrocious lyrics, but everyone hears the music. Not everyone hears the lyric.

Some people think of melody as some big thing that soars on the voice of Whitney Houston, Michael Bolton, or Celine Dion, but that's just one type of melody. Melody is hard to talk about because it's part mathematics and part spirit. But more than anything, it defines the style of a writer or writer/artist. It says who he or she is in many ways. It's like a signature or a walk that someone has. You can tell it's theirs, and you can tell when someone has been influenced by that writer. Have you ever heard someone who is going through his/her "Elton John period" or "Carole King period." Eventually, that songwriter will probably develop his own style, just as Picasso did after he learned to duplicate every major style preceding him.

Of course, most melodies are a conglomeration of influences too vast to track down. Irving Berlin always said how important it is for a melody to sound strangely familiar the first time you hear it. If it sounds just familiar enough to affect us emotionally, but not so much that it's predictable, then the melody has walked that delicate line well. Beethoven rewrote more than any of the masters and when people search their experience of Beethoven to see what was unique about his writing, they usually point to the inevitability of his melodies. Every note sounds as if it couldn't have been any other note. One wonders what his earlier drafts sounded like. Would they not have had this inevitable sound to them? And did he know what he was looking for so well, that he rewrote until he got it?

Frequently students come to me at a pivotal stage in their writing, looking for a way to make their melodies more dramatic. Everything else is there. They tell interesting stories, honestly and with pictures, on various levels. The only thing really missing is that the melodies are not marriage material. Two dates, max. But no one's gonna fall in love with these notes and chords. No one's even going to remember them after the song is over.

Without getting too hocusy-pocusy about melody being a reflection of the personality and all that stuff, I will say I've found that some melody writers play it safe. They probably colored inside the lines as a child. Now they write notes inside the chords. It never occurs to them to go outside the chordal tones for a melody note, other than a passing tone. Sometimes I point out to them some of the many songs that put the melody on the 4 of the scale, while the tonic was being played. For example, "Solitaire," the melody of which was written by Neil Sadaka. Another example is "She Believes In Me." Tension is created in both cases by the accented, held note of the hook falling on a non-chordal tone, (of course, the 4 replaces the 3 in the tonic chord when it's played, but it's not part of the tonic).

Similarly, in the rhythm of the melody, there are many options that most new writers ignore. Where to start the phrase, on what beat or subdivision thereof. And where the melody notes can fall in relation to where the chord changes. The beginning songwriter who doesn't really have his instrument down or a good feel for rhythm will write a melody's rhythm which reminds one of a new horseback rider holding on to the saddle horn for dear life. Just keep it regular and don't do anything unexpected. If you've ever sat through a set of this kind of material and lived to tell, you'll know how boring it can be.

One of the most telling things about a composer's style is the interaction of the melody and harmony. A limber, chance-taking, expert melodist can make sense out of the most unexpected chord changes. How? By the melody notes that bring logic to them. I contend that melody drives harmony, rather than the other way around. But you have to understand the harmonic side fully to write melodies that support mercurial changes like El Debarge comes up with, or Kenny Loggins, Joni Mitchell, Sting and Donald Fagen, to name just a few.

It is hard to believe that with only twelve different notes, so much variation is even possible. But look how many different faces come out of the combination of two eyes, a nose and a mouth. And a melodic style can be as individual as a family resemblance. Persistent ear training and courageous experimentation in music can help you develop a melodic signature so individual, yet inevitable sounding, that newer writers will one day be going through a "you period" on their way to their own unique styles.

34

The Rhythm of the Melody

*D*ON'T YOU THINK ALL THESE CDs we have to listen to should be tax deductible? I mean it's very important to study what's going on, not only from a lyrical standpoint and a harmonic standpoint or even a melodic standpoint. But have you also listened to that little thing called "the rhythm of the melody"?

I used to have a friend who would tap out rhythms on my arm and see if I could guess the melody. Sometimes, it would be so distinctive, I could. Try tapping out the melody to "As Time Goes By," on someone's arm and see if he/she can guess it. Or "America" from *West Side Story*. If your friends give up, hum it for them without words and they'll hit their heads like someone in a V-8 commercial. The truth is, in both of these old songs, the rhythm is very distinctive. But it's also true of most songs that the rhythm of the melody is as important to its personality as facial features are to a person's appearance. It just seems to be the part of melody that gets discussed the least.

It's an interesting exercise to spend a week listening only to rhythm of melody. Whenever the radio is on, or a CD, hone in on that one facet. See where the melody starts in relation to the count of "one." See if it's relatively on the beat or on an "and" or an "oh" as in "3-oh-and-uh"—in other words, syncopated. See if the verse differs from the chorus in this regard. Never mind the shape of the melody or its interaction with the chords right now, we're just listening for the rhythm of the notes that are sung.

Consider the song mentioned above, "As Time Goes By." The subtle syncopation is so nice in the phrases that repeat. "You must remember this," sets up the sequence that repeats rhythmically and even though they're on different scale degrees over different chords, the rhythm of that melody is the same through three phrases—actually four, but on the fourth, it's added to. So the rhythm of "You must remember this" is identical to "a kiss is still a kiss" as is the rhythm to "a sigh is just a sigh." Then when we get to "The fundamental things," the phrase continues and adds beats. Of course, the writer (Herman Hupfeld) didn't think this mathematically when it was written, but when we analyze songs to figure out what was done instinctively, it sometimes gets mathematical.

Melody rhythm can make a song sound either hip and soulful or straight and goofus. There's nothing that points up more clearly the difference between a hip rhythm and a dorky one than hearing a bad piped-in music rendition of a well-known song. You know, the kind that sounds like a nerd quantized it. Shopping can become a frightening experience when you suddenly hear a Michael Jackson tune arranged like a polka. (Imagine a Lawrence Welk rendition of "Bad" and you're starting to get the picture.) So when you ask yourself what is it that makes a totally cool melody into something you'd be embarrassed to be associated with, when the notes are identical in pitch: it's the rhythm of the melody. I've actually had people play me versions of my own songs that so radically changed the rhythm of the melody, that it seemed like a Halloween costume version of what I considered to be a designer garment. And they'd turn to me and say, "You wrote that, right?" And I'd really want to say, "No, I wrote something that sounds a little like that, but what I wrote goes like this."

Because this element in melody frequently goes unexplored or unacknowledged, people can be deaf to it and not know it. They can sing your song and change the rhythm of the melody drastically and think they're doing their version of it. Now, sometimes they can do their version of it, changing it and it's still great. Nancy Wilson recently recorded something of mine and I loved what she did. But she's a master.

Rhythm and feel and style are so intricately bound up that it's hard to talk about rhythm without dividing it into styles. But if you want to study rhythm of melody all in one album, you can get the Annie Lennox "Medusa" CD. She has songs by writers as divergent in styles as Neil Young and Al Green, Paul Simon and Bob Marley. Listen to the verse melody on the Green/Hodges tune "Take Me To The River," and compare it to the pre-chorus melody and the chorus melody. They're totally different, and yet each one is wonderful. The rhythm of all melodic sections vary tremendously. Of course, doing this drill with one of Annie's CDs is a pleasure because she's such a wonderful interpreter, whether she's singing her own incredible songs as on the "Diva" CD or other people's, as she does on the new "Medusa."

So if you get an IRS auditor who complains that you're deducting all these CDs as research, you should explain that you're investigating the rhythm of melody. After all, just 'cause it's pleasurable doesn't mean it isn't work.

35

Reading Music

*I*N ONE OF THE QUESTION AND ANSWER SESSIONS following a Campfire performance in a local high school, the inevitable question was asked: "Does someone have to read music to be a songwriter?" I had run into so many songwriters and potential songwriters who worried about their inability to "write" music, I immediately replied, "No." The student was overjoyed, but the music teachers and school administrators were not. I knew immediately I had committed a political atrocity in this high school where I was attempting to help a faltering music department. I'm actually glad I answered without thinking, because it did not cause me a moral dilemma that way. I answered what I believe to be true. I've seen so many sight readers who can't carry a tune and even more great songwriters who can't read a note. It's vastly more important, in my opinion, to have/develop a strong ear. After all, the melody is going to start in the songwriter's head, not on the paper, although it may end up there.

Of course, it's desirable to know as much as possible about music, and that includes reading it. It opens new horizons in a way that knowing how to read a language does. When you can really read scores, you can study Mahler and Mozart and Beethoven the way poets and lyricists study Shakespeare and Joni Mitchell and

Charles Bukowski. Also, reading music helps expand a writer's understanding of music theory. How easy would it be to increase your vocabulary if you couldn't read words? It wouldn't be impossible, and it would be easier for aural people than for visual ones, but reading would simply make it easier for everyone. Seeing the word helps. Similarly, seeing the melody on paper and seeing the notes that shape the chord deepen the understanding.

For a person with no ear, though, reading music is a moot point. It's like people who get bar mitzvahed by memorizing the syllables phonetically, having no idea what they're saying. I have met a number of keyboardists who can play fluently with sheet music, but they never tried picking out a song by ear. This is not a good sign. Usually if a person has a natural ear, he/she will have started playing by ear at some point. It can be developed by listening and playing what you hear, but it is a totally separate skill from the reading of music.

More often I will meet a musician who plays by ear but who has never tried to write a melody. He or she will have the consideration that not reading music would inhibit the "writing" of a song. What people may not understand is that songwriting is not "writing down songs." It's creating them. As Janis Joplin used to say in interviews, "I don't writes songs, I just make them up." Well, so does everyone else. It has nothing to do with notation. And it concerns me that people would stop themselves from doing something they may have native ability in, simply because they have never studied the process of notating or reading music.

When I was around four years old and was picking out things on the piano, after my father showed me a few chords, I had the circle of fifths figured out in a very strange way. I considered myself the C chord, my parents were F and my grandparents were B flat. I sensed the order of progression (or age or importance, in my case), but I had never been exposed to what it was actually called. All education really is in this area, it seems to me, is a codification and naming of what can be observed on their own by talented people. So if you don't know to call something a IV chord, it still functions as one. You can still recognize it when you hear a song, the way you would recognize a face in the crowd. Knowing how to play it from sheet music will never give you that recognition. It can expand it, but it's no substitute for a good ear. A student who can pick out the chords to a song he or she hears is far easier to teach than a student who can sight read like mad but can't play the chords to "Desperado" without the sheet music.

A lot of excellent songwriters have studied music when they were younger. But I find they frequently did what I did to my piano teacher. "Could you just play it once, Miss Brown, so I can hear how it goes?" And from then on, it was looking at the music, and playing by ear.

36

Playing It by Ear

I USED TO THINK A MUSICAL EAR was something you were born with and it ranged from Mozart to tone deaf and wherever you landed was where you stayed. My view of this has changed radically since I started consulting with songwriters.

First of all, I discovered that how well you can hear improves considerably with practice. It's a lot like stretching exercises. When you start, you can barely reach below your knees and within a month, you have your hands on the floor with your knees straight. Little by little, it's like that with ear training. I noticed the other day that I sat down and played a song with no trouble at all that in high school was unfathomable to me. The interesting thing is that I don't believe I've attempted to play the song since high school. It's not that I've been working on it all this time. I simply know and recognize a lot more intervals, harmonies and chords now than then. I do because I've been playing by ear all this time. And anything you continue to exercise simply gets better.

So often I'll ask a student if he or she can play by ear and I'll hear, "Oh, no." Then I'll ask if he's ever tried and he'll admit that he hasn't. Then I'll ask if he or she can sing harmony. That's a sure give-away. If the person can sing harmony—especially if he can pick out the harmony on his own—then he can play by ear. Think about it. If you can sing the notes of the chord being played, you can find it on an instrument. Some people just get overwhelmed at the idea of singing the notes and picking them out, but that's actually what playing by ear is. We see someone very proficient at an instrument simply sit down and play a song he's never heard and we think "I can't do that." We may not realize this person has spent hours sounding out chords and finding them on the instrument. We all have this picture of Mozart going to the piano and re-creating a symphony, but even at 6, he probably sounded stuff out. These were the scenes they left out of "Amadeus."

Expertise on an instrument is not easily won, but if you simply learn block chords, you can begin. If you learn the I, IV and V chord of one key—for instance, C, F and G in the key of C, there are hundreds of songs you could pick out. I'm a keyboard player, so the thought of picking out notes on a guitar—which is not laid out in a linear manner—seems disorganized to me. But playing three chords on a guitar is quite simple. You could start there. The good thing about keyboards and ear training is that the midi keyboards are transposable. By simply playing familiar fingering in a key you're familiar with, you can be triggering sounds in the key the record is in. This allows you to learn the concepts of chord function and interval relationship, without having to learn every key at first.

In Nashville, session players simply use numbers for chords instead of letters. That's what we're going for here: the relationship between the I and the IV chord—the difference in sound, no matter what key you're in. So you might as well begin thinking numbers and translate those numbers into a key you're able to play in at first. Later you can learn all the keys. But it's a little like trying to learn a vocabulary in three or four languages at once to play in every key when you're first developing your ear. If you find it easy to hear the one, four and five chord, then move on to other chords frequently heard in songs you like. Choose a new chord a week and listen for it on the radio in your car. Find it in your CD collection. It'll be like a new word you've learned. It'll pop up everywhere. Sing the notes of the chord and make sure that's the chord you're looking for. Picture the notes on the instrument, sing them and see them in your mind. I don't mean the notes on staff paper; I mean on an instrument. If you can read music, great. But this is about your ear and translating what you hear to your voice and to an instrument you can play with your hands. Soon you'll have a very large harmony vocabulary and there won't be a song you love you won't be able to play. And your own music writing will have improved immeasurably.

37

Customs & Critics & Rules (Oh, My)

*E*VERYONE WHO'S STUDIED MUSIC THEORY has heard about the period of history when the interval of the augmented fourth (or diminished fifth) was considered "the devil's interval" and was not allowed. We've come a long way, baby . . . or have we?

I'm constantly running into songwriters who want very much to be "contemporary." They eschew anything that has a sound—musically or lyrically—that doesn't sound like the week they're living in. But this can be a dangerous way to write. What was customary 40, even 20, years ago is not necessarily customary today. So the song which was very hip at the time, very trendy, will seem quite dated today, whereas a song which was simply well written, unusually beautiful and universally true may still be getting played. So bowing to the custom of the time is not necessarily a wise move, especially for a writer who has something to say. The statement may be lost in the costume of a time that will pass. It's like those album covers where the artist has on the very latest fashion. Ten years later, the artist is kicking herself with her own go-go boots, platform shoes, or Mary Janes.

A living lesson in timelessness was hearing Joni Mitchell perform as she accepted the NAS Lifetime Achievement Award (along with Leiber and Stoller and Smokey Robinson). When Graham Nash introduced her, he pointed out she always followed her own artistic path, never being governed by trends or musical fashions. He then eloquently stated that she had brought to songwriting "exquisite poetry, vision, and intimacy." She then came on stage and proved how true his statement was.

Songwriters frequently confront me with "rules" they have learned or picked up at pitches. A publisher or A&R person will tell the songwriter there are certain things s/he must do or must not do. Ever heard the one about not using the same word twice in a song? Or how about "You must get to the chorus immediately, so never have a second verse before the chorus." This is ridiculous. Obviously, there are certain conventions of songwriting that have been successful in pleasing and moving audiences for decades. It might be a good idea to know these conventions. But a lot of people who will listen to your songs are not actually creative people. They have had to memorize rules to "qualify" them to do what they do. Would you take your car to a bank teller who memorized rules about automotive repair? And yet people frequently get all upset because some totally unqualified person gave them some arbitrary rule about songwriting which they cannot implement with any success.

I had lunch with a refreshingly honest attorney the other day. He was giving me the inside scoop on a band he got signed, which every label in town was fighting over. The attorney said that he, himself, actually knows very little about songs, which—in his own words—qualifies him very well to be an A&R man. If he was kidding when he said this, he is more droll than I thought. Anyway, this band has an enthusiastic following which really likes the rhythm and energy of the band. Basically, no one on a business level knows what the songs are about or whether they're crafted well, but they did love the fact that the band filled the Roxy. The band is very careful not to indulge in too much melody, for fear their fans will think they're trying for airplay. That, in the minds of the band, would alienate their fans who would think they'd "sold out." The label who won their hearts plans to sell records without airplay, as they did for their predecessors, with whom they're going on tour.

Now, if this is all you know about the music business, you could adopt some pretty scary customs and rules for yourself: Don't be melodic, shun airplay, and assume both your attorney and your label executives know or care very little about the quality of the songs you write. The only problem with this is that there are attorneys who do know songs, many label executives consider great songs a prerequisite, and most labels need for you to get airplay to help them sell your records. So it's a little like the 3 blind people feeling and describing the elephant. Depending upon what part you're exposing yourself to, your perception from feeling the trunk will be quite different from the perception of the person feeling the tail or the rump. So until you see the big picture, it might be a good idea not to put your rules in indelible ink.

After having said all that, of course, I'm going to propose a rule of my own: Find the people who will genuinely like what you do. That's what the band I mentioned did. They had been playing for a long time and developing a following. If you're not a performer, a songwriter only, you can still develop fans— people who love your writing. This will happen for you more easily after your songs are well crafted, original and written in your own, well-honed style. On the way to that point, you will run into some "critiquers" and critics. When they tell you what's wrong or how to become stronger, try it. If it works, keep it. If, when you use it, it doesn't make your song stronger or, worst case scenario, if it simply makes you feel like quitting, it is probably bogus information.

To the person who loves dark, hard-edged metal music, a perfectly legitimate song in a softer genre will seem "wimpy." And yet, in the right place, that softer, more melodic piece might work perfectly. It's like trying to sell an orange in an apple market. It's not wrong, it's simply an orange. If the person you show it to can see the big picture, he will tell you that. If not, he will tell you how the skin is all bumpy and the wrong color. That is from his perspective—he sells apples. Is your orange really all wrong? No. It's just all wrong for him.

All of us go through periods with our writing during which there's one particular person we feel we must please. If he doesn't "hear" it, it's like the tree in the forest that really doesn't fall. If trying to please that person makes you a better writer, then go for it. But if you begin hearing a voice in your head censoring everything you write before it comes out, that person may be harming your writing—wittingly or unwittingly. Keep the river flowing. The banks will come from your own taste, artistic viewpoint and focus. All I do as a consultant is get the river to flow again for people and help with the focus. But rules are the flotsam in the river that stops the flow. Pretty soon we have a stagnant pool. And who ever heard of a person getting better as a writer if he doesn't write? Living can only do so much, and then writing has to take place to make you better at the craft.

So if a critic, a mentor, a publisher, their rules, or your own rules help you to expand as a writer, that person or rule is helping you. If you dare to reach for things heretofore not tried by you, then keep that influence around you. But if you're getting information that makes the process more baffling, more frightening, less safe to try the untried, lose them. I guess the important thing is to work on your skills until they're exceptional, then simply write or write and sing the way you naturally do it, without imprisoning your art in a trendy costume, and then find your audience. Probably your audience will find you. Then keep your focus on the listeners who like what you do, not on the disgruntled critic. He is simply not in your target audience.

38

But What Do
Strangers Think?

BEFORE I EVER HAD A CUT, my mother would listen to my songs and tell me they were a lot better than that awful stuff on the radio. I feared that meant I was doomed to anonymity. My mother didn't understand the radio and I hadn't learned to write songs. She was just prejudiced in my favor and all was hopeless. Then, by some miracle—and a Top-40 station's forcing an album cut into a single—suddenly "that stuff" on the radio was one of my songs. I was doubly vindicated. Not only was I able to pull out a title when someone asked me, "Have I ever heard anything of yours?" but also, my mother was finally happy with the pop music of my generation. It wasn't until I started playing for strangers that I learned any real lessons. More about that in a minute.

The current club scene in L.A. is just as my producer, Nik Venet, predicted it would be two years ago. Coffeehouses on every third block, and in-between, hyphenated coffee houses. Last night, I was introduced to a very charming used bookstore-coffee house. Bruce Miller, a friend and former student of mine, asked me if I'd perform in Canoga Park, California, at The Story-teller Bookstore & Cafe. He knew the owner and wanted to kick off the idea of a songwriter's night in this cafe that usually high-lights storytelling. The place is two-thirds bookshelves, filled with used books, and one-third stage and tables, where coffee and food are served. The lighting stays on throughout everything, so the audience is clearly visible to the performers.

As I sat through the open-mike segment, I was amused to see how many people were sitting there in the audience, reading books while the performers were singing. There's a sign that says books are for sale or can be read while in the store, so people pull them out and just read them at the tables. Convinced this was going to happen while I was on stage—and worse, still, that these avid readers would be visible to me, I contemplated setting my hair on fire or some other such attention-getting device. Luckily, I received some timely advice shortly before going on, reminding me to talk to the people and to think about the lyrics I was singing. Happily for my hair, that worked. They didn't appear to be reading anything while I was on. But then, I love singing for strangers. And why do I think that's so important in the first place?

If you've only sung to your friends and your mailing list, you haven't had a taste of the real world. And, therefore, you have no idea what really works. Once you sing your songs for strangers, you'll no longer be lulled by a false sense of security. If the songs have leaps in logic, the listeners' attention will wander off. If the melodies are monotonous, too derivative or inaccessible, or if the chord changes are too arbitrary or too predictable, you'll feel them drifting into their own world, far away from the one you're trying to create for them. Until you've interrupted someone's conversa-tion and changed from being an annoyance into being a focal point by the sheer impingement of your message or the universal-ity of your emotion, you haven't experienced trial by fire. If you haven't sung to strangers, you've been missing all the fun.

So where can you find some? Hanging around the local acous-tic clubs like Highland Grounds, The Roxy, Cafe Largo and Genghis Cohen in L.A. could be risky. Sure, you'll find some strangers there, but since you're required to provide most of the audience, they'll probably be largely your fans. And the strangers who do show up could be industry types around whom you don't feel comfortable experimenting.

So why not go out of town? If Siberia is too far, Los Angeles songwriters could try a club called Checkers in Torrance. I discovered this wonderful place a year after Harold Payne put it on the map. I hold the showcases of my advanced songwriting students there. There are lots of great things about experimenting at Checkers. First of all, the room is dedicated to the songwriter. Every night of the week, songwriters are showcased. So people won't come in demanding to hear "Feelings" and "I've Got Friends In Low Places." But real people do wander up; out-of-towners from conventions and all sorts of folks from all types of places. The last time I held a showcase for my students, about five pilots from an airlines convention came up and just watched from the bar, speechless for an hour-and-a-half. They couldn't understand why the room was so quiet at first; then they started listening. . . .

Another good thing about experimenting at Checkers is the gorgeous view overlooking the city. It's on the twelfth floor, and on a clear night, your songs had better be good because you have stiff competition out the window.

Some of you will live in other cities, other states. The principles still apply. Move outside your close circle. See if what you have to say and how you're saying it has an emotional impact on someone who's never heard you before. If it does, you'll know it. They'll come up to you and let you know. Then they'll move from the important rank of stranger to the hallowed halls of mailing list entry. Never miss an opportunity to add real fans to your mailing list. After all, you may have to come back to The Roxy.

39

Is There Life
Between Songs?

IT SOMETIMES SEEMS THERE'S A COFFEE HOUSE every other block and at least three songwriters in every one. That tallies up to a lot of original songs, some more original than others. It also means that opinions are being formed in split seconds all over town about the performers, their songs, their personalities, in a word, them. Those members of an audience who don't already know you are deciding very quickly whether they like you or not. They're trying to find a window to look in to see who you are. If your songs are well-crafted, honest and have emotional impact, they will speak well for you. But how well do you speak for yourself? Between songs, that is.

I used to play gay bars in the seventies, because they were about the only places you could do original material other than a full-out showcase like the Troubadour. I made some lasting friendships and discovered some of my most loyal fans by playing the Bitter End West. Eventually people would come to hear me, rather than considering me a distraction. But in the beginning, I had to work like mad to get the attention of guys whose primary reason for being there was to meet someone, certainly not a singer, and least of all a female one. But we had a lot in common, this audience and I. I wrote the title song of my first album for them, "Hollywood Town." They were a great inspiration to me. When I first started playing there, I used them as a survey to see which songs communicated and which ones didn't. My songs were just beginning to be pretty good. For the most part, though, I was an unknown performer at the piano, singing unknown material to an audience who had another agenda. They'd never heard the intros, the melodies, the lyrics. Everything was unfamiliar. So the best way I found to get their attention was to draw them into the experience of the song by talking about the subject of the song and making it their issue as well, making it part of their lives.

Obviously, I couldn't just talk about myself and how I came to write the songs, as I hear many songwriters do. That can work when you're playing to a group of people who know your material and want to know the story behind the writing. But in the beginning, they weren't fans yet. They weren't even interested in hearing songs, much less why somebody wrote them. After all, I wasn't being interviewed by Rolling Stone; I was trying to convince someone to listen who had alcohol in his veins and partying on his mind. My only chance was to make the song his story. By the time I sang the song, the patter had given him his own pictures from his own life to look at and the song had to be clear and impactful enough to carry that off till the end. Then for the next song, I had to keep him involved by giving him more common ground, more home movies from his own experience. This was actually the perfect audience for a new songwriter/singer. They didn't patronize me. If I didn't get them, they ignored me. When I did affect them, they let me know it. This trial by fire trained me so well that now the pattern is an integral part of my show.

People used to ask me who wrote the between-songs words, as if that were a whole different skill from writing songs, and that just because I was a songwriter didn't mean I could put words together well enough to speak. Granted, it's different from the structured, rehearsed words of a song lyric, but it can accomplish so much if it's done easily, naturally and with some forethought. You probably would want to have a general idea of what you'll talk about before the night of the show, but you wouldn't want it memorized. If it sounds like written material, it'll put the audience to sleep, or they'll feel like the window through which to see you is not open. They like to think they're getting a candid picture of who you are. And if you do it right, they are.

Think about your favorite performing songwriters. Do you feel you know them, even if you don't personally know them? And isn't part of that because of the way they are on stage? Not just the songs they sing, but their manner, their personalities, the way they interact with the audience and other band members . . . the way they handle unexpected things that might occur. All of these give us clues to who the person is. Are they funny? Are they down to earth and human? Are they wise and insightful? Are they, at times, profound? Are they charismatic? Are they vulnerable? Are they dynamic? A great performer will be all these things in one evening. With a well-paced show, you will see all these sides to the same person. And I've yet to see a performer who is not these things as a person actually fool an entire audience into feeling he/ she is these things as a performer. So you might as well be real. And that goes for the between songs patter, as well. The audience is going to see who you are one way or another; you might as well reveal it with honest communication in and between the songs.

You don't have to talk a lot, and certainly not before every song, but those times you do speak, make sure you let them see the real person. It can make them feel comfortable and confident that you will take them on a journey and you will bring them back safely. If you stand up and mumble something about your guitar not staying in tune, or turn to a band member and share some inside joke or take on some made-up personality that resembles bad televised karaoke, you will have lost them. Why watch you? You're not real. You're not in charge. It might not even be safe. And it's certainly not interesting. But if you talk to them, as you would a friend you're having a real conversation with about life, love, politics, the battle of the sexes, what inspires you, what pisses you off, what you observed that changed your life in some way—that will probably draw them in. And they'll be glad they came in, because they'll have met someone new that night. And it won't be the person at the table next to them. It'll be you.

40

"That Sounds Like It Belongs in a Movie"

*H*OW MANY SONGWRITERS HEAR THAT EVERY DAY? If the director or producer of the movie is speaking, then the comment can lead somewhere. But, if someone in the record industry says it, there could be many reasons: 1) He or she doesn't know what to do with the song so they assign it to a field they have nothing do to with . . . sort of like when you don't know what to do with a piece of paper you're filing, so you put it in pending; 2) The person really doesn't think the song has a chance of making it in the commercial market- place, but he doesn't want to hurt your feelings . . . sort of like telling someone his blind date is really nice and plays the piano by ear; 3) The person recognizes qualities in the song in common with other well-known movie theme songs.

This last one is, of course, the one you're hoping for, but even then, the game has just begun. Then you have to find a movie that could even remotely be right for it, have no objections to rewriting the lyric entirely to fit the needs of the film, find someone who knows someone who has something substantial to do with the movie . . . not necessarily the music supervisor who's pitching gobs of songs himself and sometimes has very little say-so . . . and beat out the 100 other songs that have come in from around the world to solve this particular dramatic problem on the screen with music and words.

I've had songs in a lot of movies, but I've never gotten one in that way. Except when producers and directors used songs of mine they discovered on their own, I've written-to-order most songs I've had in films. In the case of *The New Adventures of Pippi Longstocking,* of course, I had to tailor the lyrics. I didn't have songs lying around about scrubbing the floor on skate brushes or red-haired pre-adolescent independent thinkers. In other words, I've never been successful at sending a song in cold . . . unless it's just for a source cue, a song coming from a radio, a TV or such. And except for Amanda McBroom, who had written the song "The Rose" before it was sent to the movie *The Rose,* I don't know of other people who have found this approach too successful.

The most unusual thing that ever happened to me regarding a film was with a song I wrote with Misha Segal for a film called *Berry Gordy's The Last Dragon.* Misha and I wrote the song at the request of Suzanne Coston of Motown Productions. But when we told Mr. Gordy we were playing him a love theme song for his movie, he informed us there was no love scene and he didn't need a love song. After he heard it, he had the film re-written, the end was reshot and it was used in an emotional high point for the characters at the end of the film . . . one of the best uses any of my songs has ever been put to in a movie. But we were real lucky he was flexible enough, and independent enough, to make that happen. Today, people who hear "First Time On A Ferris Wheel" have no idea it was even from a film, but it would never have been written if it hadn't been requested for that one.

One difficult thing about writing correctly for films is getting enough information about what's needed. The song that ends a film requires an entirely different approach from the song at the beginning. In the opening credits song, you can set a mood, but you don't dare say too much. At the end of the film, you some-times have the challenge of summing up the premise of the film

. . . but it can't be too on-the-nose. And, occasionally, you have to make sense of a film that didn't make sense in the first place. ("Your music is going to save this film.") But provided you have a script or see a rough cut, and know where the song is needed, you should be able to approach the song intelligently. It's the shooting in the dark that's so trying; talking to somebody who talked to the director. It's so tempting, especially if it's a project you love, to go off and start writing before you have anything from the horse's mouth (director or producer), but for me it's been an unwise move. You end up hearing things like, "Where did you get an idea like that?" And you don't dare tell them where you heard it, because it could cost your contact his job. You just write it over, provided your first attempt hasn't cost you the pitch.

Having watched rough cuts of *Delta Force II* many times, I was looking forward to hearing Frederick Talgorn's and my song, "Winds of Change," playing as Chuck Norris drops the drug dealer out of an airplane and we watch him waft to his timely demise. It was written with that visual in mind. And even though "that song sounds like it belongs in a movie," that movie was over by the time the song started, and it played—not over the sky, the clouds and the body—but over the credits.

41

Subject Matters

*H*AVE YOU EVER SCANNED THE TITLES OF AN ALBUM, CD or cassette and decided according to the titles whether to buy it? And have you ever told a friend you just heard a song about such n' such on the radio? Subject matter matters. In films, no one would pitch an idea that was just one more story about a guy who gets the girl, loses her and gets her back. That may be what it's ultimately about, but that's not the pitch. Similarly, a song needs to come at the same old subject from a different angle. And a different subject altogether can sometimes be even more refreshing.

The ability to find subjects to write about never seems to be as hard for novelists or short story writers. Maybe that's because they're not steeped in the moon-June tradition of ancestral cliches like songwriters are. Memorable songs throughout history have always come at something from a little different angle. "Stardust," "Yesterday," "Heartbreak Hotel," "Good Morning Heartache"... these songs are all songs about lost love, but they don't say it in an ordinary way. As Nik Venet says, they take common themes and say them in an uncommon way. He further urges his writers, "The important thing for a songwriter is not to write songs that songwriters are doing already, a little better or a little worse, but to write those songs that at present are not being written." When you hear the writers he works with, you find just that.

Robert Thornburg writes about being alone at the same restaurant he used to frequent with an old girlfriend:

"Sunday Brunch/table for one
On the patio/In the sun
Huevos Rancheros/pitcher of beer
Not much has changed/since we were here
Same waitress/same menu
Same public address
Party of four/party of two
A seagull/in an azure sky
Snatches a duckling by the neck/and flies
To the rusty railroad bridge for Sunday brunch. . . ."

Ernie Payne writes:

"I was born on Coercion Street
Rocks and bottles and fists and feet
Ruled the path I daily climbed
All up hill/all of the time."

His conclusion is succinct:

"Barstool, church pew, handshake, clenched fist
I made my choices, aware of the risks.
Street muscle, blue shuffle, honed into skills
Came in real handy climbing that hill
And each step shortened the climb
As I found the voice that was mine.
Each man is shaped by his deeds;
I survived Coercion Street."

The music is comprised of open Appalachian type fifths in 12/8 time, played on a dulcimer. The effect is amazing.

When Bill Berry talks about being on the outside as a child, he calls the song "Outfielder."

"Momma said don't bother dad
 he's too busy today
And why you wanna go
 you don't like baseball anyway
And I grew up quicker then than on
 any other day in my memory.
They had blue skies
 and perfect while lines
 for playin' baseball.
I walked down behind home plate
 and hung my fingers on the fence
Thought I'd like to play the outfield
 if I only had the chance
And then a ball hit the backstop
 and finally knocked some sense
Into my dreamin.'"

One of the more unusual subjects, written about by someone who knows it intimately, is presented by Marc Corwin Bruce, an excellent songwriter who works as a public defender by day.

"He dropped the gangsta gaze
 and he looked me in the eye
He was sixteen
It looked like years since he'd seen light
The judge was going to sentence him
 for his second felony
As we sat there in the tank,
 he looked scared and lonely to me

And he said in a monotone,
'I know what's going to happen to me
I'm in Juvenile Hall
Headed for the penitentiary.'"

Due to the way this song unravels, the long applause for it at the Sunday Night Campfire reflects the fact that the audience has looked into a slice of life they might not otherwise understand. At the high schools, where the Campfire Conspiracy performs as part of GRAMMY in the Schools®, Marc is deluged with students after he sings this song, telling him stories of brothers and boyfriends and thanking him for his realistic portrayal of the subject.

When a songwriter/singer is putting an entire set or an album's worth of material together, I sometimes look at what type of song he/she is omitting. Sometimes a writer will avoid story songs, or character studies. Or sometimes a writer will have lots of stories and philosophical statements but will not have one song which is a direct communication to one person. Most songs fall into this last category, but sometimes a writer will be so intent on avoiding the middle lane where all the cars are, he or she will have a set of songs in the third person or about other people or situations or even introspective statements about him or herself, but there will not be one song where the writer simply says something to another person. When that song is written, it can give the set a different dimension entirely, just as a character description song can vary the colors of another writer's set.

Publishers will sometimes say they're looking for controversial songs, story songs, "quirky" songs, things of this nature simply because these songs stand out; they're not just another album cut which the artist can write for him/herself. What is really needed is simply subject matter that doesn't blend in with the other songs. In TV and Film script writing, you hear the term "high concept." That's something that can be pitched in just a few words and will depend less upon the execution than the overall concept. A great concept, written competently, will frequently have a better chance than a merely competent concept greatly written.

When "Black Velvet" came out, didn't you hear people talking about it? And I'm so happy "Fancy" is a hit again. It was remarkable when Bobbie Gentry first recorded it in the seventies and it's still remarkable as a cover tune. Everyone remembers the roach crawling over the toe of her high heel shoe. These two songs I believe to have excellent concepts and to be expertly written. But they're simply more memorable because of the subject matter.

Edna St. Vincent Millay once said, "Life is not one damn thing after another; it's the same damn thing over and over." Don't let your catalogs or sets be that way. Throw a streak of color in there. Don't write the same song again and again. After all, you're the only one who's lived your life. Surely there's an unusual, unique story in it. And once you have full command of the craft of songwriting, your one-of-a-kind subject matter story is just sitting there, waiting for you to write it.

42

Titles:
The Heart of the Matter

F REQUENTLY, I'VE CRITIQUED SONGS whose titles were obviously thrown on after the song was written. I will ask the writer how he/she came up with the title. He'll invariably say, "Oh, I always do those last. I just sort of look for a line in the song . . . maybe the first line or something." That's a little like getting in a car with all your possessions and starting to drive. Then when you cross the line into another state, you decide to move there because that's where you ended up. It would be helpful to know generally where you're going when you get in the car.

Titles of many of the songs we love are written before the song is written. That's not always the case, but very often the title is the first definite thing to be thought of. There may be an emotion, an impetus to communicate, a melody approach, a chord progression, even a concept . . . but the first thing to be put on paper is frequently the title. This should cut to the heart of what you want to say and condense it, capsulize it, say it provocatively, say it with a picture, a metaphor, an analogy, say it in a common expression, but whatever it does, it speaks to the heart of the matter. While we're on the subject, look at the song, "Heart of the Matter." That song could have been called "Forgiveness," or many other central themes of the song, but it was called "Heart of the Matter," because that's what it's about. The first line of the chorus is "I've been tryin' to get down . . ." but that's not a fraction as powerful as the title chosen.

Sometimes we don't start with a title, but rather find the word or phrase from the song which accomplishes what a title should. In this case, I believe a concept preceded the writing, but maybe the title itself came later, in the process of writing. An experienced songwriter will often start writing, not knowing where exactly the song is taking him/her, and in the process of writing, the story line emerges. The title will usually come later in such a situation.

Conversely, sometimes when we have a concept and a title, the song will simply develop without a firm road map of where it's going when we start. The more you focus through the title on what you want to say, and brainstorm that particular take on your story, the more supported your title will become. Every time you come to the title, it should have new meaning from the lyric leading to it. Each time we hear "This shirt . . ." in the lyric by Mary Chapin Carpenter, we know more about it and about the relationship and her feelings. Each time we hear "Lyin' Eyes," we know more about the characters. It's not just mindless repetition of a "hook." Writers, at the insistence of those who do not really understand what makes powerful writing powerful, will repeat a title until it becomes Chinese water torture. And yet at the end of the song, it means no more than it did the first time we heard it.

Students sometimes come to me with a wonderful concept for a song which I brainstorm with them. There are frequently over 50 titles that could come from the same story. Each one would lead to a different song. Deciding which angle to take, which title to develop will make the difference between a successful venture and an aborted one. That's why I discourage merely throwing the title on the song, whether before or after the concept is investigated. The title deserves a lot of thought and the lyrical road it will take you down should be looked into as clearly as possible before you devote time and energy to it. Having written songs for over 20 years makes this process almost instantaneous for me, but I shudder to think of all the titles I developed when the song I wanted to write should have been called something else.

Nik Venet talks about writing from a "concept" rather than a "good idea" because a concept is open ended and can go deep. A good idea boxes you in and is two dimensional. "Desperado" is a concept. "Achy Breaky Heart" is an idea. A title can be either one. So you might as well make the title a concept. That way, it will give you the room to deepen its meaning each verse and result in the kind of song people listen to over and over, each time getting a layer of meaning they hadn't caught the first time. All this and having it communicate something clear on first listening. Now that's the challenge! And if you've achieved all that, don't you think your song deserves a great title?

43

You Oughta ~~Be~~ Write in Pictures

WRITERS OF ALL KINDS have heard their mentors say, "Don't tell it; show it." It's certainly the rule of thumb for screen-writers. And songwriters who have been running as hard as they can to catch the wind, upon discovering this one tool, can suddenly become airborne.

"But look at this song," a student invariably says. "It doesn't have any pictures, and it was a hit." There are many answers to this. First of all, the fact that it was a hit proves nothing. But that's a discussion for another time. Secondly, established artists and producer/writers frequently get away with murderously medio-cre writing, but don't think you can. To get a song through all the people who stand between it and the artist, the song has to be memorable. The melody has to stand up all by itself and it has to accomplish that same thing for the hair on your neck. The lyric has to say something in a "remarkable" way (to quote the Nik Venet word).

Think back to the last time you either performed or heard someone else perform a set of songs which the audience had never heard before. What stuck in the audience's mind after the set was over? The pictures. Chances are, if you were the singer, you remember them coming up to you and saying "I really like the song about. . . ." And it would be something they could see. Rarely do they say, "I liked that song about how sad you were when you realized you had made a mistake about the way you had been living your life..." Vague concepts don't communicate. Even clear concepts don't communicate well in songs. Pictures communicate. I would even go so far as to say pictures capture the attention and imagination of people to such a degree, they will often excuse mounds of illogic and confusion. And as a teacher, I can honestly say it's much easier to get a "picture writer" coherent than a "concept writer" to write in pictures.

I have developed ways to train my students to translate their concepts into pictures. Although those specific exercises require some time and one-on-one explanation, I can suggest that you do a couple of other things: 1) Read poetry, especially contemporary poets like Charles Bukowski and Maya Angelou. Most poetry is full of pictures, because poets don't have the melody and voice to depend on to help communicate their message. 2) Next time you go out, imagine you have a video camera. Capture on your imaginary tape those things that would illustrate some point you're trying to make. For instance, rather than saying something about your relationship or your feelings, shoot it on imaginary video— with no sound. Find the scenes that show your story. Find the images that represent what you want to say.

In the song, "Desperado," the entire meaning is expressed in allegory. Consider how everyday it would have been had the lyric said, "You've really gotta learn to commit and feel some real feelings." We probably never would have heard it with that lyric, even with the great melody it had. But, instead, we hear:

"You've been out ridin' fences for so long
Don't your feet get cold in the wintertime
The sky won't snow and the sun won't shine;

It's hard to tell the nighttime from the day.
You're losin' all your highs and lows,
Ain't it funny how the feelin' goes away?"

It's all very conversational, but it's full of pictures. Not flowery pictures. Not painting on velvet. Just real, photographic pictures that say a lot, on more than one level.

Or take the more recent song, "Love, Me." When we think of the song, we remember the note on the tree, the grandfather at the hospital bed—like a montage.

I had a friend whose father was a fireman. He used to see people run back into burning buildings to get their picture albums. People love pictures. Whether it's in their houses or in their songs. Give the artists who sing your songs something concrete and visual to sing. And since you singer/songwriters are going to be singing your own songs over and over in your shows, you might as well have some pictures to look at while you deliver those lyrics. And if we're there, we'll get to see them too.

44

Writing in the Margins

I'M CONSTANTLY AMUSED BY STUDENTS and other songwriters who believe as soon as they can afford to quit their day jobs, they'll have all day to write songs. I don't know any songwriters who have the luxury of writing all day. The catch 22 of it is this: If you're not making a living at it yet, you're working at something else. If you're making a living at it, you're too busy to spend all day writing. Any writing you do probably takes place late at night after the phone stops ringing. So in both cases, you're doing other things a lot of the time.

Computers help, but you still have to get and input the information. A working songwriter has to be very well organized not to spend all day just doing administrative chores. The result of not doing them, of course, as some of my friends and I can testify, is waking up in a sweat wondering, "Did I ever call X back?" "When's that record coming out? Did I fill out a clearance form? Did I copyright it??" "Is my credit right?" "Did I get a copy of the cue sheet?" "Did that song or film appear on my ASCAP or BMI statement?" "If the check's in the mail, why haven't I gotten it yet?" "And who was that film producer who came to my last show, what did he say and where is his card?"

One of the most organized songwriters I know is K. A. Parker. She even organizes other people and companies. She's amazing. I have had to hire people to get me organized. It's actually much more important than I ever wanted to admit. Haven't you ever jotted down an idea for a song and then lost the piece of paper? Multiply this times 1000 and you begin to get an idea of how confusing life can be when it really gets hectic—people asking you for songs for projects, juggling collaborators and demo schedules, keeping track of the people you meet day to day or at events or your own showcases. My computer data base is full of people with the word "who?" in the comments field. I simply have no idea where I met them or why I have their cards. Now I code every card when I get it.

The closest I ever came to being able to write all day was at the beginning of my first publishing deal. I wasn't a recording artist yet, so I only had to write songs and make demos and my publishers frequently organized the demo sessions. Within a few months, though, I was with a record company too, so things got more complicated. Live performances, recording sessions, touring, interviews etc., etc. I had a manager, an agent, an attorney, a business manager, a publisher and I still had to provide them with what they worked with—songs, information, figures, etc. This left very little time to write songs. I wrote in the margins of my day. That's all I had left.

Even when a writer isn't also an artist, it can get very hectic and time consuming. The accountant can only handle what you give him or her. So you still have to organize all the finances including watch-dogging every source of income to make sure you receive what you're supposed to. For instance, is your song which they used in that TV movie really a source cue (coming out of a radio or other source) or is someone singing it on camera or over credits? Did the music editor or supervisor list it correctly on the cue sheet? You get paid by ASCAP and BMI according to how it's listed on the cue sheet. And the difference in performance royalties is often worth tracking it down.

Then there are the totally unexpected interruptions to "normal life" like one that happened to me two years ago, and I'm still hassling with it. A student of mine walked in one night and said "I thought you wrote 'Ain't No Way to Treat a Lady.'" He went on to explain he'd seen a Helen Reddy's Greatest Hits CD and that someone else's name was listed as writer. It was the same writing team whose song appeared two cuts down on the CD. Apparently a typist's eye fell on the wrong information as he/she was typing up the label copy. If I divide the amount of time I've spent on this into the money I'll make, I'll probably end up making less per hour than the typist who erred in the first place. I had to hire an attorney to write the record company to ensure that the Harry Fox Agency had issued the license properly. They had. The company assured my attorney on re-issue, the credit would be corrected. So I thought it was handled. Then, over the next two and a half years, I noticed this particular CD number never appeared on my statements from the publisher of the song. I called them and they'd allegedly never gotten paid from the record company, and they didn't even realize it. After many cross-country calls, I've now been informed it will appear on my next statement. But I couldn't help wondering . . . what if I hadn't caught this? The publisher may never have gotten paid. I would never have gotten paid. And this is just one example of one cut on one album.

My writer friends and I laugh about how much of our time is actually spent on administrative details of this nature. Naturally when you're extremely successful, you have someone else doing a lot of this for you. And sometimes you never really know all the nightmare they're taking care of for you. But sometimes I wonder if stars like Elvis really knew what Colonel Parker was doing in his name. It's very important to surround yourself with a trustworthy team who will fight your battles for you courageously and ethically.

But mostly, you have to do it yourself. You have to keep track of those people you meet and what they want or need from you. You have to be aware of where all your songs are—the ones you're writing, the ones you're pitching, and the ones that are in film and TV projects or on someone's album, being translated into other languages or just sitting on your work tapes waiting to be demoed. Henry the VIII is rumored to have patted a youngster on the head and said, "You look like a nice little boy. Whose child are you?" and the boy said, "Yours." Sometimes you have so many songs in various stages, you'll be at a restaurant and you'll hear something start playing that sounds strangely familiar. Then you'll realize it's yours and you'll be genuinely surprised to hear it. That's when the people at your table will invariably say, "It must be nice to be a songwriter and be able to sit around all day, just writing songs." If you're smart you'll smile and agree. Maybe you'll even add, "Yeah, it really beats working for a living."

45

Writing in Space

I'M ALWAYS HEARING COLLEAGUES AND STUDENTS say they're not writing because they don't have the time. And I know that can seem to be a real problem. But consider, if you will, the following premise: Songs are not written in time; they're written in space. A flash of inspiration can come to you at the strangest times and places. Usually it's where you're not prepared to write it down and when you don't really have the time to develop it.

That's one reason keeping a journal is so helpful. I've always considered the muse a bit perverse, anyway. I mean why do we get all our best ideas where there's no pencil? Like in the shower or in bed. So all the preparation you hear about designed to invite the muse—sit in this chair, write every day, schedule writing sessions, quit your day job—it's all ritual. The truth of the matter is, you can write anywhere anytime, with no time devoted to it, in the margins of your day or in the middle of another activity. Of course, once you get the ideas that come in the flash, some time is needed to develop them. But if it's something real that is screaming to be said, it'll write itself. No matter what you may have planned, that song's going to get written. And your schedule will just have to adapt. You may have to pull over to the side of the road, or stay up all night or be late to your appointment. But that baby's coming out.

So what is this "space" we need to write a song in? I will attempt to keep this discussion down to earth, even though it's not a down to earth kind of thing. The space I'm talking about you can't put something in—it's not physical. But it's absolutely real. You hear people say every now and then "I just wasn't in the space to do that." That's the kind of space I'm talking about. Some people call it head space, but I don't think it's in the head. But then that's another discussion.

How do you get this space? One way is to get rid of the stuff that's taking up the space you do have. You know how good you feel after going through a closet and throwing unusable garments out? Well, writing space is created by going through and throwing stuff out too. A mundane example would be going through papers that have been piled around pulling at your attention. Of course, you may argue that if you had time to go through the papers, you'd have time to write. But remember I'm contending that you don't need time to write, you need space. So try going through the papers, until when you walk through that room, nothing's pulling at your attention. Now you have attention to pay to other, more creative matters. Other things can hold your attention—worries, secrets, fears, your general baggage. As Nik Venet says in his workshop, "Your luggage may be designer luggage, but you still need to get rid of it." I won't get into the benefits to the personality of this kind of housecleaning: there are enough benefits to one's writing to be discussed.

Have you ever noticed that while you're on vacation—away from all the daily attention grabbers and routine—you get all sorts of ideas? Space was created from throwing out all the normal day-to-day activities. Pretty much anywhere you can be where a realization could occur is space making. A great speaker or an inspiring book can do it. I notice it regularly at the Nik Venet Workshop where people have such regular and frequent realizations, they don't notice when they leave that the tops of their heads are missing. They have lost, weekly, more and more misconceptions about songwriting, performing and the music business. They don't understand why they go home and write songs. It's done in all that space that was left after the false information was blown out.

Just as getting rid of negative things can create space, so can adding positive ones. Now, the positive experience may not be what the song ends up being written about, but it can create the space in which any song can be written. For instance, doing something you feel really good about—helping someone and being of service, doing a wonderful concert, meeting a new person, falling in love, etc.

You know how good you feel after giving or seeing a great concert. You could stay up writing all night, whereas at that time of night on any other night, you might feel tired or uninspired. Since not everyone does concerts, let's take the example of being of service. Do you remember a time you were able to do something someone really needed? Maybe you helped a friend get through a problem, or worse yet, move from one apartment to another—something totally selfless. You know how good you felt? Every time I see a student break through something in his/her writing or solve a problem in a particular song, I get a burst of space along with him or her.

Remember when you fell in love? You might have had the busiest schedule in the world, but you found time to think about that person, didn't you? And didn't ideas come rushing into your head like a broken-dammed river? And you'd write them down while you were brushing your teeth or on the freeway. You didn't clear out your schedule to write that. You wrote it in the space created by that heightened affinity you felt for the person.

Another space creator is having a burning desire to communicate something. Lots of songs are written after a painful or frustrating experience. Usually, there is something you really needed to say or do which never got said or done. That undelivered communication will want to come out with the force of a love song in the first burst of love. It needs to be said. It will nag at you and create its own space in which to get written. When Mickey Newberry was asked why all his songs were sad, he said that when he was happy, he was out having a good time. And when he was sad, he was home writing. Maybe that's why many of the positive love songs are still written about longing for someone the writer cannot be with at the moment. Richard Marx says to his wife across the sea, "I'll be right here waiting." If they'd been together, the song might never have been written.

Every new father and new mother I know has written a song about the experience of feeling a huge burst of love for a new baby. And who could be busier than a new parent? Love creates space. It's as simple as that. And in the space, we write.

So the next time your songwriting friends give you that lame excuse about time, tell them about the final frontier. Tell them to clean their apartments. Take a vacation. Get their hearts broken. Have a baby. Fall in love. (Not necessarily in that order.) After all, the space for a great song could come from it. And aren't we all accused at one time or another of doing it for the songs?

46

Playing the Symbols Well

WHY CAN'T WE BE LIKE DOLPHINS and just send the message without symbols? A dolphin wants to send "apple" to his friend and the next dolphin receives "apple"—the concept, not the word for the concept. If people were like that, songwriters might be out of a job. As it stands, though, we're really needed to say all those things other people would like to say to each other and can't quite do it.

Songwriting really is a language. And the better you are at it, the better the recipient gets what you're trying to say. So how do we ensure that the other person is going to get the actual message and not get tangled up in the symbols of the message? Well, first of all, learn to speak the language you're writing in. Learn to express yourself clearly when you're simply talking to someone. That's a start. Have you ever heard a jumbled up song and then heard the person explain what he was trying to say and it's just as confusing as the song? Some people don't really know how to say something clearly when they're just telling you a story, much less put it in a song clearly—translated into their second language (songwriting).

But let's consider our control group to be songwriters who do know what they're saying, who do know how to communicate clearly when they speak. Now whether they can get that message across, in song form, is another matter. As I've said in many other articles: pictures . . . pictures . . . pictures. Give the listener something to look at. Show it, don't say it. Let the listener in on your movie. That's pretty much the mantra of every writing coach, whether s/he is discussing songs, screenplays, short stories, novels, whatever. In fact, bring all the senses in. Bring in taste, hearing, touch, the works.

Recently, I heard a wonderful explanation and suggestion by Nik Venet at his ongoing workshop. He suggested that everyone take one of their lyrics and get two highlighter pens. He said to highlight in red all the concrete words—words that refer to things which can be perceived by the senses. Then he suggested the writers highlight in blue all abstract words—anything conceptual, not concrete. Obviously, there should be a balance between the two and sometimes by doing this, it's clear that there's not. When you look at a page filled with blue and only one or two dashes of red, the problems in the song become much clearer.

What is done with the concrete words and images, then, is what determines whether the writing is first or second level. I maintain that metaphors build a song down, rather than out. They give it that other dimension. "The Dance," by Tony Arata (recorded by Garth Brooks), for instance, could be viewed as a visual song, with a lot of concrete—a good balance. But what gives it depth is that "the dance" is metaphorical. It stands for much more than simply a dance. This happens more often than not in great songs. There will be a meaning, which is very clear on a literal level. Then you get to go to the next floor down, which is the real meaning, symbolized by the concrete words.

Where writers often get into trouble is that they hurl metaphors like a mad scientist might mix ingredients. There are all sorts of abstract ideas being presented by symbolic pictures but before the logical thread of one is followed out, it switches to something else. Sometimes that's called "mixed metaphors." And that's easy to spot. Perhaps a more subtle version is the use of one metaphor which simply doesn't compute. When you follow the logic of that symbol, it would not lead to the conclusion you want, so you write yourself into a corner. Using metaphors, similes, analogies, and other symbolic literary conventions without thinking each one out logically beforehand is like a novice taking apart your computer and rewiring. I don't think so.

But once you get the hang of it, using concrete words in a way that says something symbolically can deepen the meaning of what you write immeasurably. First we will be moved by the literal story, or we will at least be intrigued. Then we will want to look into it further. Metaphor can give the listener gems to discover hearing after hearing. Every time I hear "Desperado," or "Blackbird," or Joni Mitchell's "The Beat of Black Wings," I discover something else about each song. I also discover something else about songwriting. And, as in the case of all great art, about myself.

47

Cleverness and Subtlety

WHEN I FIRST STARTED WRITING, I heard cleverness was a good thing. But I mostly heard it from other songwriters, who were at the same level I was. Slowly, I started noticing that cleverness calls attention to itself. I look back on some of the lines I wrote on my first albums and I'm a little embarrassed by the cleverness. It definitely calls attention to its own "smartness" and takes the listener out of the experience, much the same way that a less than subtle acting performance will break the verisimilitude of the film or play. When I watch Robert Redford, again, in *The Way We Were*, I appreciate the subtlety of his underplaying. The line between powerful performance and histrionics is a thin one, walked delicately by the great actors like Olivier, Pacino, Dustin Hoffman, Meryl Streep and others. But sometimes, when I look back at old movies, or even at new ones, I notice the acting, and that bothers me. I want to forget the acting. The same goes for songs. I want to forget the writing and just have the experience when I hear a song. Cleverness for cleverness's sake doesn't add meaning. It distracts.

The melody on which a lyric rides can help it to be subtle. In fact, melodies have been saving lyrics for generations (usually when the artist is the writer; otherwise the lyric might keep it from getting cut altogether). Imagine if Seal's "Kiss from a Rose" had a melody that wasn't dark, haunting, medieval and highly unusual. People would listen and go, "Say what?" Seal, himself, was honest enough to admit in an interview he has no idea what his lyrics mean, so with a less charismatic melody, he might be left hanging out to dry with those words. Melody can save the day somewhat for a clever lyric, as well. In "One of Us," by Eric Bazilian, when Joan Osborne gets to "'cept for the pope maybe in Rome," it's at the end of a serious song with a strong, serious melody. It's not a "comic" melody. That would be a disaster. *Who's Afraid of Virginia Woolf*—another old play/movie—was deadly serious, but I laughed harder than at any comedy. If the context is real, everything works better. So if you're going to throw cleverness in a song, it had better be serious, ironic, sardonic or something with an edge. Otherwise you have slapstick. Alfred Johnson is skilfull at this edge, for example, in his hilarious lyric to "W2," which is cradled in a soulful boogie piano and constant reminders of the dark, sinister intentions of the IRS. The discovery that he played it for them during an audit just adds to Alfred's audience's shocked enjoyment when they hear him live.

Shakespeare's non-comic characters even punned, but he cloaked it in seriousness and irony. For instance, Shakespeare has a dying character say, "I am a grave man," and he has Hamlet says "I am too much in the sun," punning on "son," when he addresses his murderous step-father. This is meaning laid between the lines. If no one gets it on first reading or hearing, fine. It's not pie-in-the-face. It's the square root thereof. Subtlety is pastel colors, not bright neon.

It's very tempting for a naturally witty person to be clever when s/he writes. But the kiss of death for a witty line, in conversation, is to hear "ba dum bomp" afterwards. You know you blew it when that happens. And it can happen in a lyric. Listen to country radio for a while. See what happens when a song comes on you've heard before that ends each chorus with a punch line. If it doesn't have an underlying seriousness or bite—if it's just clever—I bet you change the station. "I've heard that," like a joke you've heard before. But if there's irony in it that comes from a real life emotion, then you'll hear it again and again, because the punch line delivers a feeling.

A few years ago, the amazingly acerbic and brilliant Marie Cain was reviewed as being like X (a famous singer/songwriter) but more subtle in her satirical songs. Ms. X read the review and screamed across an entire room, "SUBTLE??!! I'M SUBTLE!!!" The anonymous singer is actually one of my favorites, and a great artist in her own right, but even though she is droll, she is not as subtle as Marie Cain, who is a master at it. If you've heard her, you've probably noticed she's a walking lesson in how many layers of meaning you can get in one satirical song. "Friendly Fire," a lyric she wrote for Steve Schalchlin (who wrote the melody) for his show, "The Last Session," is staggeringly witty. And against the black backdrop of the subject matter, it shines like the gem it is. In the song, she parallels troops being killed by friendly fire to the toxic effect of medicine that's supposed to be protecting the body by fighting the disease.

When you've seen the sharp edge of a master's blade, it's hard to appreciate the blunt attempts at cleverness in any art form. It's the difference between a Maya Angelou poem and a Hallmark card. As Nik Venet put it recently in his Workshop, "Cleverness is a clown in disguise." And I suspect he was not referring to Picasso's "Pierrot."

48

Starting with the Song

I HAD ALWAYS HEARD, BELIEVED AND TAUGHT that record production starts with the song. But I'd never understood it at such a real level as I did this last month, in the studio, recording my new CD, which I had been writing for nearly five years. Nik Venet, my producer, is a champion of the song and his every move in a recording session is to protect and project the song and its content.

Early in the sessions, Shel Talmy, who was recording next door, came in to talk to Nik Venet. He told the story of how Venet helped him get the attention that later led him to produce The Who and David Bowie. He also mentioned the article that listed Shel and Nik as two of the last hands-on record producers who see the big picture, who are not simply engineers, players, or over-seers, but song people who see the entire album as a piece of clay and follow it to a complete sculpture. How this is done became clearer to me during the weeks that followed.

When the musicians arrived, Nik Venet explained to them the concept of the album and passed out lyric sheets along with separate chord charts. By the time I walked back from getting tea, they were ready to listen to the songs. They were aware it was not simply a chord chart session, that the entire song was being played—even the lyric. I would play and sing the song at the piano and they would listen and follow the chart. Then we would rehearse it on tape. By the third or fourth take, and sometimes sooner, these legendary players, some of whose work I've adored for decades, were creating takes. Having played alone for a number of years, writing, performing and even recording, I was transported hearing the parts they came up with.

In one particular case, on the song, "Chinese Boxes," I heard some rather amazing things coming from Abe Leboriel's bass. On playback, I realized that not only had he captured the darkness of the mood, but he also added Oriental overtones. "I'm playing the lyric," he said in his inimitable manner and accent. Without exception, the other consummate musicians (Dean Parks, Craig Stull and Tim May, and Dennis Budemier on guitar and Jim Hugart, alternating with Abe Leboriel, on bass) all commented on the content of the songs, the melodies and the lyrics. And the playing reflected their understanding of what the songs were about. So my fear that a group of triple-scale musicians were going to get together and read chord charts, with no attention to the lyric and melody content of the songs themselves, was totally unfounded. By the time the basic tracking sessions were over, the songs had all been discussed in detail. And I had the best tracks of my career.

A real producer is like the director of a film. He or she gets the script as perfect as possible before shooting and casts the supporting players (musicians, singers). Similarly, Nik Venet, worked with me on getting the songs written for the last four and a half years. Right after we finished the "American Romance" album, I started writing the songs for the "Rosebud" CD. More than once, I would receive a phone call at some ungodly hour, and I would hear Venet's voice or read a fax from him telling me to read something, watch something, do something. In each case, it would lead to a new awareness which frequently led to a song. This collection of work is not just one angst ridden entreaty after another (as some of my earlier albums sound to me now). There are songs about Marlene Deitrich, Frida Kahlo, references to two films ("Citizen Kane" and "Casablanca"), two books (*The Snow-*

goose and *A Tree Grows In Brooklyn*), rodeo riders and the 90-year-old couple who lives upstairs in my duplex. And, in place of angst-ridden entreaties, Venet challenged me to turn the flashlight on the darkest corners, to stop complaining and start revealing. I believe I did that.

So I feel as if I've come full circle. The very thing I've been teaching has been taught to me. The song is what it all starts with. My vocal and keyboard performance came from the song. The musicians' playing came from the song. The background vocalists sang the songs. Since they were all songwriters in their own rights, they really got into the songs: Gary Floyd, Jenifer Freebairn, Jannel Rap, Corwyn Travers, Scott Wilson and a duet with Steve Schalchlin. And last but certainly not least, the producer known for not leaving a fingerprint did everything necessary to stay out of the way of the song and make sure everyone else did. He showed off the song through what was not done as much as by what was.

I can hardly wait until next week. I never dreamed when I heard "Ode To Billy Joe" and " Bridge Over Troubled Waters," I'd have strings by Jimmie Haskell. But Nik Venet has asked Jimmie to arrange strings on hundreds of albums and promised me when we made "Rosebud," there would be Jimmie Haskell string arrangements. At a time when lyrics and melody are once again becoming as important as poetry, film and visual art, what could be better than being a songwriter?

*A*ppendix

I

*P*ublication *D*ates

The dates of original publication for each article are provided here for historical perspective on when certain references were made. In many cases, artists, books, and songs were mentioned before their later, widespread success. For these reasons, the chronological context may be of some interest to the reader.

Appendix

2

Chapter Topic Guide

While studying Ms. Schock's material for my own sake, I made notes about which topics she discussed in each article; this made it easier for me to go back to a particular subject as different issues would come up in my writing. Her insights continue to inspire me in new ways every time I read them. I hope that this topical guide will help you find the *Becoming Remarkable* passages you want to work with at any given moment.

—Naomi Healing

Writing correctly for films
> *Chapter 40: "That Sounds Like It Belongs in a Movie"*

Writing melody first
> *Chapter 30: Words or Music . . . That Is the Question*

Writing lyric first
> *Chapter 30: Words or Music . . . That Is the Question*

Writing Layers of Meaning
> *Chapter 46: Playing the Symbols Well*

Appendix

3

Lyrics

rosebud

> orson tells the story so well
> and despite the lack of snow in texas
> i see myself
> sledding
>
> and every time i watch it again
> i see parts of life
> that i've always been
> dreading
>
> the sweetest moments
> fading like snapshots
> in old trunks
> of faces no one living quite
> remembers
> but crushed between the pages
> of a well read book of poetry . . .
> a rosebud.
>
> some believe that time is no friend
> while others insist that they've learned
> how to bend it
> their way

well, i see a mansion
with hallways and big rooms
with footsteps
and mem'ries
but only one that really lingers
and safe within the pages
of my favorite book of poetry . . .
a rosebud.

maybe i lost my sled later than kane did
but it's gone, all right
just the same . . .

so i do what i do every day
and i do what i do
'cause i've found a way
to do it

oh, but when night falls
and clocks stop and dreams come
i'm back there
and sometimes when i
least expect it
his arms hold me
and over all the pages
of all my books of poetry . . .
rosebud.

Published by: more future schock songs (ascap)

patsy cline

he cries in his house
she cries in hers
is each mile between them
a blessing or a curse?
the noise was too painful
but the silence is worse

when he cries in his house
and she cries in hers.

she paces her house
and he paces his
reliving the locked eyes
the quick touch and the kiss
who made up their story
to end it like this?
with her pacing her house
and him pacing his.

and patsy cline keeps fallin' to pieces
and they let her 'cause she does it so well
her heartbreak is clean
not caught in between
the long road to heaven
and the fast road to hell

what she now calls her house
they used to call theirs
their best times between them
are now tables and chairs
the flood of old mem'ries
catch her unawares
when she cries in her house
that used to be theirs

and patsy cline keeps fallin' to pieces
and they let her 'cause she does it so well
her heartbreak is clean
not caught in between
the truth and what the truth cannot tell

he danced into her life
she waltzed into his
they dreamed of what could be
and seldom of what is
so there will be moments

when they more than miss
when he was in her life
and she was in his
when he was her life
and she was his.

Published by: more future schock songs (ascap)

fool that i was

lookin' back on my dream world
i had it all i
wouldn't trade with any other girl
what do you call it?

some call it fantasy
and some place that's part of me
still calls it how it oughta be
but that's the way i fall . . .

fool that i was
i thought the moon rose from your fingers
fool that i was
i hung my plans on every word you said
i loved you without reason like a baby does
and no one misses more than i do
the fool that i was.

lookin' back on our sweet life
so many filters
i can only see the light
and that's the killer

how our diamond shines
between the lucerne palm trees i'm there
just about all the time it's
shining on me still . . .

i let the roses die
they didn't come from you

when they ask me why
i'll say that's what they do

fool that i was
i thought the moon rose from your fingers
fool that i was
i hung my dreams on every word you said
i loved you without limits like a baby does
and no one misses more than i do
the fool that i was
fool that i was
fool that i am.

Published by: more future schock songs (ascap)

i'm gonna hold you to that

underneath the hunger and the anger and the pain
and the fear of losing everything in one long rain
i've noticed that the heat of passion only sets the stain
of your love . . . in my blood . . . runnin' through my veins.

we were standing in the kitchen
as i recall
you were looking at my eyes
and i was looking at the wall
i told you i was scared to take the fall
and you nodded

i told you about my father
and the fact that he had died
that i had never replaced him
as hard as i had tried
you said that you would live
and i cried
and you nodded

i'm gonna hold you to that
i've got to know that it's true
i don't like fading to black

i thought i told you
you tell me things'll be fine
that you're not ending the world
i need to hold you to that
i need to hold you.

we were arguing in the driveway
about security
and you started talking money
and i tried to make you see
my pilot light was still your heartbeat
and you nodded . . .

where i come from, a nod is like a yes
and yet the way you give me answers
it's just anybody's guess
and yet i think i heard you confess
when you nodded . . .

(chorus)

Published by: more future schock songs (ascap)

dreaming of casablanca

don't get me wrong
i'd never want another lover
your touch has held my fragile heart for so long
but somehow these days
i feel like a sister, mother
and something in my mind just wants to move on

but i decided when i fell in love with you
this time that's not what i would do

yet i'm dreamin' of casablanca
there's longing in the rain
pictures of casablanca
are coursing through my veins
day by day i'm a good girl

in this thelma and louise world
but at night i dream of casablanca

it's petty i know
when the world is full of real problems
and through the daylight hours i'm in there fighting
but the goin' gets slow
and i wonder if i'll ever solve them
and there's a hunger of the heart that's in here hiding

when the nighttime brings those shadows to my bed
rick and ilsa drift into my head . . .

and i'm dreamin' of casablanca
there's longing in the rain
pictures of casablanca
are coursing through my veins
day by day i'm a good girl
in this thelma and louise world
but at night i dream of casablanca

at night i dream
the same dream
that weakens the seams
of everything
that really matters

must i always test the wings of sacrifice?
won't you just gaze into my eyes?

'cause i'm dreamin' of casablanca
i'm longing in the rain
visions of casablanca
are coursing through my veins
day by day i'm a strong girl
in this thelma and louise world
but at night i dream of casablanca
please come with me . . .
to casablanca.

Published by: more future schock songs (ascap)

worn around the edges

it feels so good
it feels so right
it took me years
to reach tonight
but here i am
maybe a bit the worse for wear
and here you are
and maybe you don't care

that love is all that i can give you
i wish that i could give you more
but the love i have to give you now

is better than before
it's just a little worn around the edges
got a patch or two where it's been sewn
but i hope you'll take it like you would a gift
made by loving hands at home.

it's been so long
i've walked so far
but now i'm back to where you are
i've been through fire
i've been through emptiness and shame
i've changed a lot
but i love you the same

and love is all that i can give you
i wish that i could give you more
but the love i have to give you now
is better than before
it's just a little worn around the edges
got a patch or two where it's been sewn
but i hope you'll take it like you would a gift
made by loving hands at home.

it feels so good
it feels so right

it took us years
to reach tonight.

words and music by arthur hamilton & harriet schock
Published by momentum music/more future schock songs (ascap)

last love song

i was flyin' a mile a minute
never stopped but always intended to
sad but true
i didn't count on you.

i had made a firm decision
unaware of what this collision could do
my heart just grew
i didn't count on you.

you say i'm your last love song
you bring me such sweet romance
well, i'll be your last love song
if you'll be my final dance.

when love used to move to winter
i'd find some passionate interlude
just to get me through
i didn't count on you.

i guess you've changed forever
the list of things i would never do
you know it's true
i count on you.

you say i'm your last love song
you bring me such wild romance
well, i'll be your last love song
if you'll be my final dance
i'll be your last love song

if you'll be my final dance.

Published by: more future schock songs (ascap)

it flies

it can start as fear of the unknown
especially when we spend our time alone
but love stood in the doorway that night
like a wild bird poised before flight

it flies
it flies
it soars over burning skies
it dives
and sails
and its spirit never fails.

it's not the way you thought that it would be
yet everything's in focus and you're free
so you watch the black tipped feathers of the bird
and you never have to say a word

it flies
it flies
it soars over burning skies
it dives
and sails
and its spirit never fails.

everything you dreamed of doing
suddenly you can
everything except to understand . . .
how the snow goose came to find your home
and why you feel so blest at times
at times so all alone

it flies
it flies

it soars over burning skies
it dives
and sails
and its spirit never fails.

it wails
and cries
but its spirit never dies.

Published by: more future schock songs (ascap)

a tree grows in brooklyn

the concrete is poured
on top of the boards
yet the seeds are stored and
waiting
a breeze comes along
and whispers some crazy song
and the camera cuts to
green growing through the grating

it grows out of neglect
and reaches for respect and
admiration
it's a celebration
a rose blooms where nobody's lookin'
and he knows
a tree grows in brooklyn.

where there is no time
where there's only space
where human hands don't touch
and lovers don't embrace
still there's a sign
and those who miss it must be blind
as it slips out over the bible
and dances to its own survival
his whisky is poured

her sober heart's bored
her dreams have been stored and waiting
a room full of smoke
can't soften the broken glass reflection
of a youth that's fading.

where there is no time
where there's only space
where two souls can touch
in moments without embrace
there's living proof
that spirit is the only truth
as it slips out over the bible
and dances to its own survival

the hungry heart turns
the broken heart learns
as ritual burns and crashes
love gives her the chance
to live inside a glance
and stella steps from blanche's ashes

a rose blooms where nobody's lookin'
and she knows a tree grows in brooklyn
yes, they know a tree grows in brooklyn
i've been there . . .
a tree grows in brooklyn.

Published by: more future schock songs (ascap)

over and over and over

the television
looks like it's from the fifties
except that there's a cable in the back
and he sits in his special chair
half awake and half aware
that she is in the room somewhere
that is his pivotal fact

the photograph
is clearly from the thirties
with smiling features of the bride and groom
and my eyes pan from it to them
it looks like her, it looks like him
and the spark of love has not grown dim
it lights up the room

they're headed where their
parallel lines will finally meet
he only sought to rule the world
to lay it at her feet

over and over and over
she steals his heart
that is her art
and over and over and over
she chooses him
and they both win . . .

and when his knees
are just not up to walking
well, she goes down the stairs to get the mail
and if i'm dressed and quick enough
i sometimes go and take it up
as if this long abiding love
were my holy grail

their bodies don't obey them
in this inning of the game
and yet the look inside their eyes
is constant and the same

over and over and over
she steals his heart
that is her art
and over and over and over
she chooses him
and they both win.

Published by: more future schock songs (ascap)

marlene

in the city of the angels
where nobody gets blue
we have a vague recollection
of someone like you
but we couldn't make the funeral
we had so much to do
marlene . . .
i think that was your name.

yes, our stars are best at shining
with their backs against the wall
and we sometimes see them broken
and sometimes see them crawl
but we're certain to forget them
if we don't see them at all
marlene . . .
i think that was your name.

we have our garbo
coat and scarf and shades
and norma jean
her mystery never fades
we have princess grace
with her perfect face
why do we need you?
you broke the rules . . .

in your custom-made tuxedo
you were hot from head to toe
they say you walked away from hitler
and toured with g.i. joe
but politics are boring
it was so long ago
marlene . . .
i think that was your name.

we have our garbo
coat and scarf and shades

and norma jean
her mystery never fades
we have princess grace
her supermarket face
why do we need you?
you broke the rules . . .

the procession was in paris
and another in berlin
there were diplomats from places
that you had never been
but there was no one from the movies
i guess you weren't a friend
marlene . . .
i think that was your name.

Published by: more future schock songs (ascap)

okay, you win, i give up, (you're right, i'm gone)

if i can get this old pen to write
i'll get it all written down tonight
i'm runnin' pictures of me and you
knowin' now what i've gotta do
this'll save you some breath
on how it all oughta be.

day by day you pontificate
on all the people you've come to hate
and here i'm sittin' at three a.m.
aware at last that i'm one of them
i'm only sorry tonight
it took me so long to see . . .

but i say

okay, you win, i give up, you're right, i'm gone
you stand your ground so well,
i must be movin' on

you were a wizard in every way
but the man behind the curtain has had his day
okay, you win, i give up, you're right, i'm gone

ignore the place where the ink just ran
i don't expect you to understand
that even now as i lose my pride
my heart's still tryin' to take your side
and so i turn up the light
to drive the mem'ries away
and i say

okay, you win, i give up, you're right, i'm gone
you stand your ground so well,
i must be movin' on
your blood was blue, your suits were grey
but your feet were 100% pure clay
okay, you win, i give up, you're right, i'm gone

on and on, the clock keeps turnin'
doesn't it know we're over now?
nearly dawn, all bridges burnin'
that clock's sure ticking loud . . .

(chorus)

harriet schock and jannel rap
Published by: more future schock songs (ascap)

you are

if we'e gonna be children
for the rest of our lives
why then pretend to be husbands and wives?
and if we're gonna be blinded
by the tiniest light
why not admit that we prefer the night?

do we take out our toy swords and guns?
or put out the white flag and run?

you are
my harbor
my knight in shining armor
and i wonder sometimes if you know
all you are

you are
the air
this drowning fool's last prayer
and tonight i would kill to be where
you are.

if we're gonna stay hungry
for the rest of this meal
i will confess to you how hungry i feel
and if there's anyone listening
while this tree tries to fall
please make a note it was my heart that made this call

and sometimes the demons take charge
and deal everyone the wrong cards

but you are
my harbor
my knight in shining armor
and i wonder sometimes if you know
all you are

you are
the air
this drowning fool's last prayer
and tonight i would kill to be where
you are.

Published by: more future schock songs (ascap)

rosebud

produced and directed by nikolas kos. venet
re-mix produced by jeffrey casey and joe robb
"i'm gonna hold you to that" produced by jeffrey casey
evening*star record productions
co-producer: nik venet, jr.
conducted by: jimmie haskell
engineer: joe breuer and joe robb
assistant engineer: kennedy herkel and joe breuer
recorded live & mixed at cherokee studios, hollywood, ca
mastered by: tom baker at future disc systems, west hollywood, ca
photography: henry diltz
art direction: art ziegler
print production: ivy hill
production executive: michelle fox
production supervisor: sue crawford
associate producer: mitch santell
executive producers: margaret marston & marie siroonian

thank you marlene dietrich, frida kahlo, paul gallico, orson welles, l. ron hubbard, dan woodruff, claire mcfarland, louise hamre, pamela lancaster johnson, susan watson, zonnie bauer, tom lane, loy whitman lane, marie cain, jimmie haskell, janna hines, michelle fox, earnestine jefferson, johnnie mae crawford, arthur and elizabeth schoch, the austin schochs and epprights, norman meullen, neal springer, fay and arthur towvim, sarah mcmullen, peter mainstain, debbie schuch, bobbi cowan, joe viglione, jane woodward elioseff, genevieve vaughan, marie siroonian, margaret marston, eric larson, peter jameson, scott wilson, steve wagner, sarah kim wilde, steve jackson wilde, bruce larsen, bill berry, ernie payne, robert thornburg, jim dean, leslie claussen, lee shartzer, marc corwin bruce, sue crawford, marc staenberg, brendan okrent, beverly houston, barbara mcmillan, kim oliver, steve szmidt, hillah cohen, rosa lavarreda, merrill's music and john frederick nims.

I would also like to thank the evening*star supporters, sam & karen amato, lois tilley and dennis tilley, timothy schomer, lynn andeen, mary bittinger, gerd bjorke, virginia bodie, stuart & joan estra, wyatt garfield, john & gayle jensen, stuart & susan macdonald, barbara najar, peter smith, gaile sickel, jim burk, kathy koeing, diana marie, bruce singer, joan palmer and merethe reklev. Special thank you to joan tourtellot and schlomo zadok for performance photos.

dedicated to sandra, kay and karen killough for their tenacious support, love and faith and to nik venet who is always my inspiration.

harriet schock, 4/2/97 and 5/15/98, hollywood, ca

PLAYERS

Musicians:
    Dean Parks - Electric Guitar
    Dennis Budimir - Electric Guitar
    Marty Rifkin - Pedal Steel & Mandolin
    Craig Stull - Acoustic Guitar
    Tim May - Acoustic Guitar
    Ken Empie - Acoustic Guitar
    Abe Laboriel - Electric Bass, Guitaroon
    Jim Hughart - Acoustic Bass
    Joe Lamano - Electric Bass
    Suzie Katayama - Cello
    Daryl S - Viola
    C. Douglas Lacy - Accordion
    Joel Derouin - Violin
    Harriet Schock - Piano
    Jeffrey Casey - Drums & Acoustic Guitar
    Gary Floyd - Piano
    Over and Over, Worn Around the Edges
    Jeffrey Casey - Arranger
    I'm Gonna Hold You To That
    Conducted by Jimmie Haskell

Backup Vocals:
    Corwyn Travers
    Jannel Rap
    Jenifer J. Freebairn
    Scott Wilson
    Michelle Fox
    Gary Floyd
    also guest vocalist on Patsy Cline and Last Love Songs
    guest vocalist Steve Schalchlin
    on Worn Around The Edges
    courtesy of Bob-A-Lew Music

SONG LIST/AUTHORS

    1. rosebud - words & music by harriet schock - 2:55
    published by: more future schock songs (ascap)

    2. patsy cline - words & music by harriet schock - 3:55
    published by: more future schock songs (ascap)

    3. fool that i was - words & music by harriet schock - 3:02
    published by: more future schock songs (ascap)

4. i'm gonna hold you to that - words & music by harriet schock - 3:36
published by: more future schock songs (ascap)

5. dreaming of casablanca - words & music by harriet schock - 5:05
published by: more future schock songs (ascap)

6. worn around the edges - by arthur hamilton and harriet schock 2:57
published by: momentum music, more future schock songs (ascap)

7. last love song - words & music by harriet schock - 2:51
published by: more future schock songs (ascap)

8. it flies - words & music by harriet schock - 3:50
published by: more future schock songs (ascap)

9. a tree grows in brooklyn - words & music by harriet schock 5:02
published by: more future schock songs (ascap)

10. over & over & over - words & music by harriet schock - 3:23
published by: more future schock songs (ascap)

11. marlene - words & music by harriet schock - 2:52
published by: more future schock songs (ascap)

bonus cuts:
12. o.k. you win, i give up (you're right, i'm gone) - 4:07
words & music by harriet schock & jannel rap
published by: more future schock songs (ascap)

13. you are - words & music by harriet schock - 3:18
(bonus tracks from - american romance: all about eve, lady suite and
the coyote) used by permission, godsdog records,
nik venet record productions
published by: more future schock songs (ascap)

Index

About the Author

*H*arriet Schock was born in Dallas, Texas, where her father taught her to play the piano by ear at the age of 4. She studied piano privately through grade school and high school, and she wrote her first song in the seventh grade. She received a B.A. in English but continued writing songs, mostly special material for skits and school events. Shortly after college, she moved to Los Angeles and signed a contract with Colgems-EMI as a staff writer. In 1973, she recorded her first album for 20th Century Records, containing her song, "Ain't No Way to Treat a Lady," which became a hit for Helen Reddy and was later nominated for a Grammy.

Harriet currently is a gold and platinum songwriter and a recording artist with five solo albums. She was voted best new female artist by *Cashbox* magazine, received a Dramalog Award for her live show, and has garnered extremely favorable press for each album she has released. (Some of this press may be viewed by going to the eveningstar1.com website.) Smokey Robinson, Roberta Flack, Helen Reddy, Lee Greenwood, Johnny Mathis, Syreeta, Carl Anderson, Gloria Loring, Vikki Carr, Manfred Mann, Mireille Mathieu, Letta Mbulu, Nancy Wilson, and many others have recorded her songs. She also wrote "Dreaming" which was recorded by Jodi Benson *(The Little Mermaid),* a favorite among *Little Mermaid* fans. With Misha Segal, Harriet co-wrote "First Time on a Ferris Wheel" for the Motown film, *Berry Gordy's The Last Dragon,* as well as all the songs for *The New Adventures of Pippi Longstocking,* and the animated *Secret Garden.* Her songs have been featured in numerous films and TV shows.

213

Harriet taught songwriting for two years at USC in the undergraduate program and has lectured, taught, and been published in songwriting magazines nationwide. She has been teaching songwriting for twelve years, one-on-one private lessons, group classes, and correspondence courses. She has been writing about songwriting for seven years. Her CD, "Rosebud," produced and directed by the legendary Nik Venet, is an illustration of the principles and philosophies discussed here.

Harriet Schock can be reached by e-mail at hschock@relaypoint.net or see her website at www.harrietschock.com